A Year íi
a Faei ɔ ·ˑιιυη

Sage Weston

www.capallbann.co.uk

A Year in the Life of a Faery Witch

©2001 Sage Weston

ISBN 186163 139 1

Cover design by Paul Mason
Cover and internal illustrations by Lin Bourne

Published by:

Capall Bann Publishing
Freshfields
Chieveley
Berks
RG20 8TF

Dedication

To my Mother...................whoever she is, wherever she may be

and to all those who seek to walk the hidden path in the
ancient Faerie ways.

Lydia
Allison

There is valere
in every life, and
every moment of each day.

Alan

Contents

Also by the same author, published by Capall Bann:

Eternal Priestess

The Magical Year

The spiritual life is not an easy one. The millions of people who walk blindly from the cradle to the grave sensing little more than their own bodily needs will never know the anguish of other, more sentient beings, who walk beside them. During one incarnation or another the soul awakes and, like a fretful baby, agitates to be allowed to grow and follow its' destiny. This 'child' must be identified and fed and, like all good parents we must learn at times to submit to its' will. As it grows so we see a mirror image of ourselves and, if properly nurtured, we will eventually integrate this creature into our lives. At this point we will have realized that it is our soul that is craving attention, our own spirit that is growing and leading us into higher realms. And so, upon recognition of this fact, we join forces and move a further step up the evolutionary spiral. The tortuous path that leads to this point and the fundamental changes that are incurred as a result of the personal insights gained, tell us more about the meaning and purpose of life than could previously have been imagined. The path is an individual one, tailor- made to fit, we all learn to walk it in the end but it may take many lifetimes. Realisation of one's true path may be reassuring or shocking but sooner or later it will present itself.

When I realized that I was a witch I was both appalled and bewildered. Every unpleasant connotation surged into my mind and I felt insulted beyond words. And yet, this was the only term that could fit what I had always felt in the depths of my soul, the only explanation for my 'eccentricities' and inclinations, the only way to explain the far memory I had of a life very different from the one I had now, a life of remote freedom and communion with natural forces. For years I searched and researched both inwardly and outwardly, tested the water, drew many blanks and frequently got my fingers burnt. Still my destiny beat on my soul and I made some dramatic changes. Time and again I jettisoned unwanted cargo, fine-tuned my ideals and looked within. More had to go, and, often with a heavy heart, I unburdened many outgrown relationships, broke through yet more psychological barriers and faced a future stripped to the bone.

The study of witchcraft came easily and gladly and I thirsted for more. A natural progression led me to search for magic from any culture I could find. An Egyptian Mystery School offered a good foundation and a future but I still hankered after the Western Mystery Tradition. Faerie drew me and I turned my attention to Celtic myths and Irish folklore probing the truths behind the tales, looking for the magical ingredient that would provide inner transformation, trying to find my way through the labyrinth to grasp the ethereal and the transitory. What I was looking for had to touch the depths of my soul and once or twice this did indeed happen as I stumbled upon an aspect of an ancient and perhaps forgotten culture.

The way to Faerie is through witchcraft; the two are first cousins, one more remote than the other. Whilst the witch may live on the outer realms of a settlement, by the boundary, Faerie lies beyond that, in the wild places - on moors and hills, by still pools, mountain streams and inaccessible glens. The two worlds intermingle but witches still have a foot in this realm whereas Faeries only visit, choosing times when mortals are absent, the gulf between us all having grown too wide to allow for more intimate contact.

Both witchcraft and Faerie were once an integral part of society but urbanization has driven them away. As we look with dismay at the heavy price we must pay for materialism many are drawn back to a simpler lifestyle and erstwhile witches emerge from male domination to once more seek their heritage. Drawing heavily on intuitive knowledge and perhaps guided by unseen hands, the Old Ones who have not returned to this earth - we move gingerly forward, recovering lost arts and thrilling to the call of the ancient wisdoms buried in the land; the standing stones, the sacred groves, the holy wells and the glories of the night sky. In simplicity we find profound truths and an innocent happiness; in solitude we learn to know ourselves and our part in creation; in healing we are healed.

This book is a 'grimoire', a journal of one year in the life of a Faerie Witch, newly accepted into the Craft but in fact re-awakened and re-directed, looking at the world through the eyes of enchantment, seeing it as it should be, re-created anew every day.

Included are a few idle snippets of information, insights and rites, ideas that have impacted or realisations gleaned from lifting a corner of the veil. May those who follow this trembling path gain from the following account, perhaps only a little comforted, perhaps inspired, perhaps just mildly amused at one magical year in the life of a Faerie Witch.

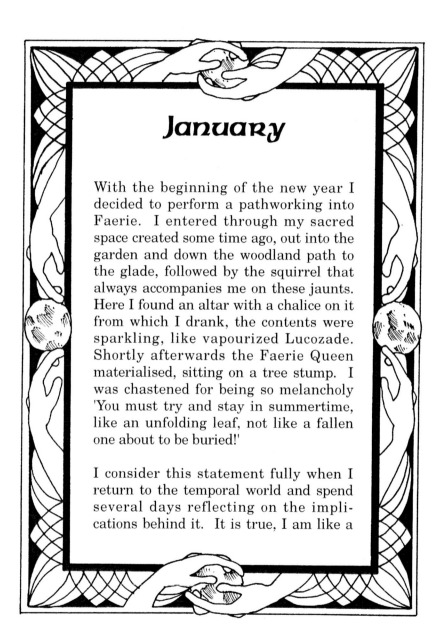

January

With the beginning of the new year I decided to perform a pathworking into Faerie. I entered through my sacred space created some time ago, out into the garden and down the woodland path to the glade, followed by the squirrel that always accompanies me on these jaunts. Here I found an altar with a chalice on it from which I drank, the contents were sparkling, like vapourized Lucozade. Shortly afterwards the Faerie Queen materialised, sitting on a tree stump. I was chastened for being so melancholy 'You must try and stay in summertime, like an unfolding leaf, not like a fallen one about to be buried!'

I consider this statement fully when I return to the temporal world and spend several days reflecting on the implications behind it. It is true, I am like a fallen leaf, withered and lifeless, disillusioned by the world around me and sour at finding myself alienated from a society which has become so shallow and unimaginative. It is, however, the middle of winter and the earth pulse has yet to quicken. Gazing up at the night sky I observe with satisfaction that the Pleiades have passed the mid-heaven point and are on their outward journey towards extinction in April. When the Spring comes, when the days lengthen and the Lady returns, then I will re-emerge too and become like a fresh green leaf, bright and joyful.

....

Meanwhile I consider other plans that have lain dormant throughout the dark days. Soon the cleansing tide will be upon us and new beginnings will mean much pruning and discarding. Old festering problems must be addressed and some decisions made, the brooding must cease and the nettle be grasped; without further prevarication I decide I must initiate myself back into the Craft. For too long I have postponed this step, unsure of my commitment, my suitability or my aptitude. In spite of efforts to dismiss my inclinations and to avoid a label with mixed implications my thoughts return time and again to witchcraft, haunting and taunting me, reminding me of some forgotten obligation which I am quite unable to articulate.

In my daily life I laugh with colleagues, chat easily to shop assistants and smile politely at garage attendants. I move unobserved through mainstream society, playing my part discreetly, attracting no more attention than is essential. But at home in my cottage, alone and undisturbed, I grin happily into the darkness as I put out the empty milk bottles - the night is full of Faerie Beings and I sense their presence, allies and old comrades. The morning sun crawls over the rim of the earth and I greet it with outstretched arms and a prayer of thanks.

Spring, and I sense the moment of ignition, amidst the beating rain or gusting winds there is a pause, almost indiscernible, and in that hovering hiatus a motor whirrs and a spark flashes and life begins once more. The sap begins to rise and mine rises with it, expectant, buoyant and energised once more.

Late August and the earth is baked to a deep golden crust. The last of the corn is cut, hedgerow fruits are ripening. 'I can do no more' cries the Goddess of Plenty. I hear the groan amidst the mellow summer sunshine and sense Her turn and compose Herself for sleep, drained and depleted. She has gone for another year, unrecognised and unacknowledged by so many.

The moon beams in her fullness and I gaze in wonder, as always. The stars dance above me in labyrinthine patterns, offering symbols and mysteries I cannot fathom. The green hills call to me and the green lanes tantalise me - something profound stirs within and I grope to remember bonfires on hilltops, trackways to long-vanished settlements, dewponds and mighty oaks, beckoning woodlands and enchanted buttercup meadows - behind and beyond it all the 'call of the wild', elemental, ghostly and compelling. The ancient cry that has followed me down the years, wailing for my attention, recalling dimly-held memories and primitive urges. I am piecing together fragments of a heritage, undeniable, powerful roots embedded in my soul. It is the Craft that I identify, the Craft of the Wise, the forgotten world that once held me in thrall; the gateway to faerie, the missing link between the world of mortals and the world of the Sidhe. I must return to the source and reclaim my birthright.

....

It is still deep, deep winter. Midnight blue skies give way to bright cold mornings, the land silver-coated and crumbling beneath the frost, bacteria and unwelcome bugs destroyed for another year. Survival is still precarious and I feed bread to the birds who swoop down from their icy perches, having long since consumed the berries and living now on human handouts. I crack the ice on the birdbath and soon it is full of abluting sparrows, so cheerful in spite of the famine.

Inside I stoke up the woodburner. Peat blocks filched from the nearby moor have kept it in all night but now a log makes a brighter blaze and I pack it well with coal nuts to form a new heart. My fire burns all winter long and by this time of year a deep warmth has built up and permeated the cottage. I rake out the ash and take it outside in a bucket to add to the cinder path which now almost reaches to the back gate.

The cold weather grips us all day and by mid afternoon a thick fog has descended. I fling more bread out for the birds but the gloom has sent them home to their nests and I retire indoors to sit by the fire, feeling that the world is at a very low ebb and myself sinking in parallel. Early to bed, I pad myself with blankets and pillows; all is inert, both inside and out, I join the rest of the animal kingdom in hibernation and achieve the 'little death'.

....

The new moon, the Lady, shines brightly in the clear winter sky, a sharply defined crescent, starkly opaque against the deepening blackness. I catch a glimpse of Her at supper time, my arms full of sticks. At this time of year, when all else in nature is dead She is a particularly welcome sign of renewed hope. I down-tools and raise my arms in worship, bowing deeply three times.

'Holy be each thing
Which She illumines.
Kindly be each deed
Which She reveals.'

Having greeted Her warmly I resume my tasks. In one
moon's time, just after Imbolc, I shall re-initiate myself into
the Craft; suddenly I feel there is much to look forward to. I
glance across the meadow to the willows standing starkly
along the perimeter. Are they too filled with renewed hope?
Solemn, immobile, they remain untouched; it is hard to
remember their lilting summertime movements after so long.
As I gaze into the far distance I see a large ball of vapour form
and slowly revolve, a globe of mist, the size of a haystack. I
watch incredulous as it winds its way across the meadow
towards me, a few feet above the ground. Then, just as it
approaches the fence on which I am leaning, it turns and
wheels its way towards the far hedge, easily passing through
and moving slowly out of my vision. I stare in disbelief,
glance back towards the willows, expecting to see a re-
occurrence, but find only the empty, moonlit field. Heaving at
the log basket I return indoors to note my experience -even I
won't believe this in six months time. Later I realize that I
observed this phenomenon through my third eye, my nightly
meditations which have recently been focusing on this feature
have clearly had an effect.

The living room glows in the firelight and I sit in the rocking
chair contemplating the sinking logs, my mind a million miles
away, there is no sound to interrupt my thoughts, just the soft
shifting of ash as they disintegrate, television and radio have
no place here, I am wedded to the land, not the human race.
At this low point of the year I have learnt to embrace the
darkness and my brain has ceased to crave any form of
stimulation. I no longer yearn for the Spring but have
succumbed to the rule of the God. In the gloaming it is easy
to slide into trance and it seems appropriate to visit the Dark

Goddess. I have made her acquaintance already in the past but now feel that as I embark upon a serious study of the Craft I must ask for assistance. I duly sink into semi-consciousness, the cat on my lap as always, but within a short while finding myself unaware of her presence. I approach the Dark Goddess via a cave that leads to an underground pool, lit with concealed lights of blue and green, mirrored by burning tallow-dipped rushes mounted on the cave walls. I walk down carved steps into the pool, warm water and billowing robe giving a sense of buoyancy. Before me on a dais, carved out of the rock face, sits the Dark Goddess, draped heavily in black from head to foot and veiled to the waist, She sits severely upright, in the 'Egyptian position' - impressively forbidding. I wade through the water towards her and bow as deeply as possible. She makes no sound nor movement so I offer my plea for guidance in the ancient wisdoms as I consider initiation. Still she remains motionless and eventually I turn to go, but she raises her hand to halt me and promises me a guide or sentinel in that rather gruff voice of hers. I thank her and depart. When I leave the pool and turn back for a last look she has gone. I am soon rocking my way back to reality in the rocking chair, the cat now a dead weight on my lap. Let us hope my promised guide proves to be worthwhile.

....

The moon is full in Cancer. It is too damp and cold to perform much of a rite so I merely stand in the garden bathed in moonbeams offering a brief prayer to the Goddess. It is clear and breathtakingly beautiful.

....

The days are horribly dreary, although beginning to draw out now, sunset is well after 5:00 p.m. In the stillness of the cottage my psychic senses are opening out and I am now aware of anyone trying to contact me by letter or telephone. The postman brings no surprises and I have my answers ready as I pick up the receiver. There is such deep peace here and I eke out the days knowing that soon I will be active and energetic once more.

....

My supply of kindling needs replenishing and this means a trek to the woods with a sack or two. In spite of a few rays of sunshine the woods are dark. All is dead here and I am ankle deep in leaf mold. There are sticks in abundance, sodden and slippery - but I soon have two sacks full and take them home to dry in the outhouse; the coal bunker is still half full but there is little peat left. After dark I drive out onto the moors where mountains of granulated peat, ready for bagging, rise black against the sky. The ground is thick with mud and the car slides wildly but in the headlights I see broken blocks lying at the foot of the peat mountain. The boot will only hold half a dozen and I cram it full and drive up to park on the river bank which runs in a straight line across the moor. Here my tiny rowing boat lies under wraps for the winter. All is secure, the river has subsided after the recent floods and my boat has remained high and dry throughout. In the distance the multi-coloured lights of Abbeybridge twinkle, the Knoll stands sombrely against the night sky and the deep black moor slumbers under winter stars. I mentally surround my boat with a blue light to keep it safe for a little longer and turn the car for home. No animal nor bird cry breaks the silence, I am the interloper in this solid wintry scene - true 'north' is here, blue-black skies, mountains, midnight and monoliths.

....

The moon has darkened and I feel myself withdrawing in sympathy, outside the skies are still grey and the weather is squally. I have a free day and decide to spend it in seclusion and fasting. My big feather bed is warm and comfortable and I lie quite still beneath the quilt, trying to quieten my brain which is telling me to get up and perform a few chores. After half an hour or so it ceases to chatter and I achieve a state of suspended animation - the silence and stillness of 'Faerie'. I drift in and out of consciousness, images rise and fall before my third eye and a deep purple light appears. I doze and wake, the clock face turned to the wall and the phone unplugged. All day I lie there in a trance-like state until the light goes from my bedroom window and I venture downstairs. It is four o' clock and I drink a cup of coffee, light in head and body, then return to bed. Quickly I am able to recover my earlier state, my brain thoroughly subdued, my mind surrendered to a higher reality. I feel a timeless sense of belonging - to whom, to what? I sleep a little and then arise once more, happily drained and re-charged, sleepily relaxed. It is eight o'clock. Another cup of coffee and a sandwich, then it's bedtime again and I sleep until morning, purged and re-created.

With the new moon I begin to make plans.

Emergence

Winter tides with all consuming force
Sweep darkly on their pre-determined course
Sighing resignation tinged with dread
Man's journey through inertia lies ahead.
Necessary maybe, worn out molds
Must break, reform and meet the deadly cold
The crawling hand of midnight proffers death
And all submit their final gasping breath.
In caverns, vaults and deeps beyond the void
The strong are tested, weakness is destroyed.

A light arises on the eastern skyline
Mere shimmer yet a reassuring sign.
In drowning depths of darkness comes the hour
When hope is born and nurtured into flower.
The pivot turns and human hearts respond
Reprieve has come again from far beyond.
We glory in the long awaited birth
Of sun and stirring life within the earth.
The planet masquerading as a tomb
Regenerates to serve as nature's womb.

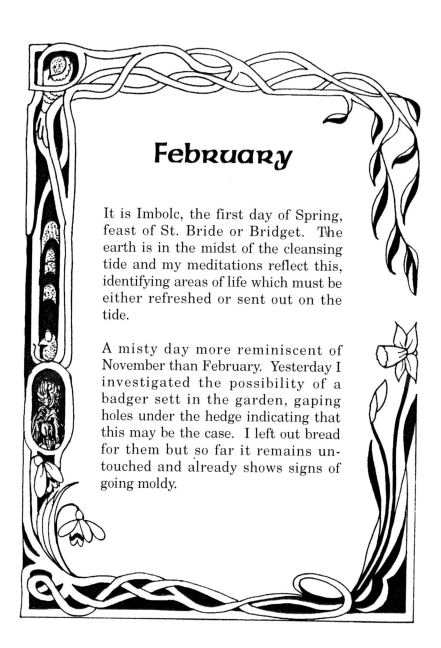

February

It is Imbolc, the first day of Spring, feast of St. Bride or Bridget. The earth is in the midst of the cleansing tide and my meditations reflect this, identifying areas of life which must be either refreshed or sent out on the tide.

A misty day more reminiscent of November than February. Yesterday I investigated the possibility of a badger sett in the garden, gaping holes under the hedge indicating that this may be the case. I left out bread for them but so far it remains untouched and already shows signs of going moldy.

'Every day and every night
That I say the genealogy of Bride
I shall not be killed, I shall not be harried,
I shall not be put in a cell, I shall not be wounded...
No fire, no sun, no moon shall burn me,
No lake, no water, nor sea shall drown me.'

There is no evidence of Spring outside but I am able to find a handful of snowdrops with which to decorate an altar. Utilising the traditional blue and white theme I find a piece of white cloth and a couple of blue candles, then, adding incense, a bowl of water and a dish of salt I mark the four quarters. In spite of the dampness I nevertheless set my altar up on a brick plinth outside and perform a small rite at sunrise. I forgo a robe due to the low temperature but cast a circle and invoke the elements in my own homemade way.

Then, standing in the centre, I call upon the Lady and welcome Her back into the world with a short poem of my own creation. Communion is bread and wine as always. I am not particularly uplifted by the rite but, as I return the left overs to the earth when it's all over, I feel a great sense of satisfaction and a duty happily completed. Now the long winter is passed and the Lady's green hand will soon bless our land, plans appear more promising and a glimmer of hope shines over the horizon.

....

Bitter cold with a heavy mist that lies all day. Cocooned in a pointless no man's land of the soul, neither vibrant life nor annihilating death.

....

Damp and sodden, rotting oak leaves underfoot. Brambles are dark green, shaggy willow herb saturated with dew braves the winter out, not a single new shoot anywhere, everything is waiting for Nature's starting pistol.

....

A feeling of hopefulness. The sun is out and the wind is gusting - sunshine and shadow; the catkins entice us with their waving yellow fingers. Plants, hitherto drooping disconsolately now stand tall and look more purposeful. The Goddess stirs. The sap is rising and I feel mine arising in accord. Occasional sunbeams through the window illuminate the grime of winter and I put Spring cleaning on my agenda for next month. Meanwhile I am gathering together implements and writing a ritual for my forthcoming initiation. A friend has given me a glass chalice as a gift and a short sword found last year in a junk shop will make a useful athame when scoured with steel wool and polished. Whilst wandering around the local market I find a small silver plated goblet for only £3.00 and an interesting dish with a snake motif - these will be ideal for the communion bread and wine. I already have a wooden dish suitable for 'earth' and another inscribed with symbols in which, if filled with sand, would do to burn incense in. A crystal bowl that belonged to my Grandmother completes the set.

I have planned initiation for next week's full moon which seems as auspicious as any other time; in anticipation of this I spend the evening consecrating my implements, wrap them carefully in some old black silk which I knew would come in useful one day and store them in a chest in the bedroom ready for the big event.

My daily meditations at this time are turned towards the forthcoming initiation. I have spent the usual twenty minutes each evening focusing on the path ahead, no longer questioning my decision but opening myself up for guidance. No great insights come my way, nor does my dream life offer doubts or awful warnings, I must assume that I have been given the green light from the Goddess. I have scoured all the esoteric books I can obtain for information on self-initiation and have compiled a liturgy suitable to my circumstances, combining traditional forms with my own original ideas. The result is an interesting mixture which I hope will reflect my sincerity and open the gates to the Astral World.

....

The moon is full in Leo and riding high in the sky, clouds pass across Her face from time to time but She remains untouched, beaming down in triumph. Tonight I will re-initiate myself as a Witch, the living room has been cleaned in readiness and my tools brought out from the bedroom chest. After dark I arrange an altar out of a draped coffee table and place all implements in position. With the curtains drawn and the fire banked up, the room already has a cosy, otherworldly glow. I am a little concerned about the magical name I have chosen - 'Clover' - it seems a little precious and nondescript. However, as I have already started to use it in small ways it is too late to change and when all said and done it does remind one of flower-strewn English meadows.

I bathe in salt water to cleanse my psychic field as well as my body then massage oil into my skin until I am scented and glowing. My hair is loose and well brushed and I have on the necklace and bracelet that I keep for magical rites. Naked, I stand in the doorway of the living room composing myself, the fire has sunk to a bed of embers and, as a consequence, the room appears darker. I light more candles and carefully place my script on the altar, remembering at the last minute to fetch my reading glasses.

The moment has come. I mentally discard all that I can pertaining to the past, thrusting from me the years of turmoil that has brought me to this point. With a deep breath I walk towards the altar ready to dedicate myself to a new form of service. I pick up the athame resting there and start to describe a circle.

As rites go my re-initiation can only be summarised as a disaster. Although I have some magical experience I am defeated here by the lack of light and space. All goes smoothly until I anoint myself on the brow and a drop of oil dribbles into my right eye producing the most acute burning sensation. Unwilling to break the circle in order to bathe it and about to reach something of a crescendo in my dedication I attempt to read the script by candlelight with one streaming half closed eye and the other malfunctioning because my glasses slip off my nose. It occurs to me that I may be permanently blinded in one eye and sniffle as well as I can in order to produce the teardrops that will soothe the pain and cleanse my eye. Without clothes there is no where to hang glasses nor stuff a handkerchief and I feel I must present a very woebegone figure to the Goddess and God. In desperation I discard the script half way through and offer a spontaneous supplication.

'Accept me as priestess and witch O Lord and Lady of Life - your servant Clover!' I cry.

A moment later, clearly and steadily into my mind, come the words 'Clover Wild Crow'.

I stop, bemused. A magical name, I have been given a complete magical name, my plea has been heard and I have been accepted. Tears at last fill my eyes, the oily one and the plain one, they drip off the end of my nose and I sniff and snort in gratitude. Joyfully I conclude the rite with communion and open the circle, stumbling through the gloom to the bathroom for some eye drops and a handkerchief. I have not been blinded after all and when, clad in my dressing gown, I survey the scene by the fading firelight I breathe a sigh of relief. 'Clover Wild Crow' - not a bad magical name, in fact quite suitable. A touch of the Buffalo Plains perhaps but never mind, I have been accepted in the astral realms and that's good enough for me. I have a good blow and wipe my eyes.

....

In view of my new allegiance it occurs to me that it would be a good idea to investigate the elements more fully so I give some thought to the possibility of doing that this year. I have for some time longed to walk one of the ancient trackways and this is perhaps the opportunity I need for studying earth and air. In the Spring our village hosts a Firewalk so that would allow me to contemplate fire and in terms of water, well, my new boat can assist me here. I view the future with anticipation. Not for me the complex dynamics of a coven, I shall remain a solitary witch, walking my own path, making my own discoveries.

....

Once more the moon is dark, it is cold with flourishes of late snow. After a miserable day at work I am glad to be indoors. There is little in the larder but I am accustomed to plain eating and manage a sort of high tea. Then, after stoking up the woodburner and unplugging the phone, retire early to bed seeking my own scrap of monthly seclusion along with the Lady. I drift off, pondering on a solution to the tension at work and sleep deeply and dreamlessly, craving oblivion.

I awake in a somewhat drugged state feeling as if I have been 'told' something that now eludes me. However, I have solved the problem in the office, I will do a spellworking for peace, nothing else has worked and I need employment, so I shall call on the Gods for assistance.

As I rise, sunshine greets me and I can hear the welcome sound of woodpigeons cooing from the treetops - winter is truly over.

The Sap Also Rises

At early dawn the call at last goes out
A murmur pulsing through the blinding earth
Passed low and trembling reaching nature's kin
Announcing Spring's renewal and rebirth.

Easing leaf and fur from winter torpor
Gently shaking each from dreamless depths
Thrilling with a voice of expectation
Breathing vital hope with whispered breaths.

Feral creatures dimly sense the summons
Surging sap ignites the verdant flame
Whilst mortals keep their deathly fireside vigil
The signal is obeyed as life is claimed.

A lacy shawl of green is cast on treetops
Early flowers waft wildly to and fro
Then birdsong fills the air with joyful chorus
And man emerges ready for the show.

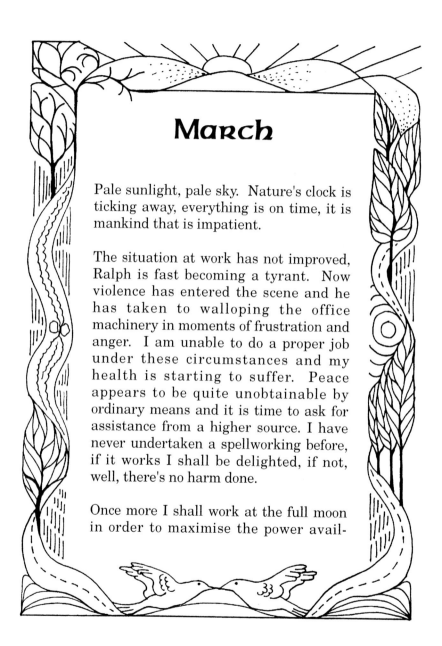

March

Pale sunlight, pale sky. Nature's clock is ticking away, everything is on time, it is mankind that is impatient.

The situation at work has not improved, Ralph is fast becoming a tyrant. Now violence has entered the scene and he has taken to walloping the office machinery in moments of frustration and anger. I am unable to do a proper job under these circumstances and my health is starting to suffer. Peace appears to be quite unobtainable by ordinary means and it is time to ask for assistance from a higher source. I have never undertaken a spellworking before, if it works I shall be delighted, if not, well, there's no harm done.

Once more I shall work at the full moon in order to maximise the power available, meanwhile I must design it according to the required specifications. Ralph has his own pen which he uses especially for signing letters and cheques, it wouldn't be difficult to borrow it overnight. If this pen were to be consecrated in some way, allowing for peace to flow when it is used then perhaps the atmosphere in the office would slowly improve. I have no desire, nor should I want, the power to bring about enormous changes, just a little respite from his towering rages which don't do anyone any good, least of all Ralph himself.

Now that the main theme of the spell has been established I spend a happy evening by the fireside making more detailed arrangements concerning the appropriate venue and the correct powers to be invoked. I decide to approach the Lord and Lady of Life for their help and of course invoke the elements to join me in the circle. Ralph is a peat producer and the business is, naturally enough, situated on the peat moors. It therefore seems appropriate to work this spell close by the factory on a disused piece of ground near the river bank. The moon will have risen by twilight and, as I often spend time wandering along the river bank, my presence will not be unduly alarming should anyone appear. As for the actual ritual, well it won't take long and I can shield myself from prying eyes behind a peat stack. Beyond that stretches the moor, a wasteland at first glance and quite uninhabited except by deer and badgers; nobody walks these forgotten paths and Neolithic trackways anymore. I doubt if I will be seen by anyone.

....

I am pleased and a little excited at my developing plans. There appears to be little need to write an elaborate invocation, I am quite sincere in my request and will speak from the heart. My experience of the initiation has taught me to keep things simple and it seems best to carry this theme through into the spellworking. Of course a robe will be impossible but I shall take my hurricane lamp and hope that it serves in place of candles, otherwise I have all the equipment I need to hand. I am now able to face my days at work with greater detachment, knowing that there will ultimately be a change for the better. In my lunch break I make a quick survey of the proposed site and find a suitable area to cast my circle. All I need to do now is arrange to borrow the pen.

....

Tonight the moon will be full in Virgo, it is mild and the sky is clear as sunset approaches. I stand at the wide office window watching pink vapour trails dissolve in the sky and admiring the apricot coloured clouds shifting and reforming in the west. The sun is a large fiery orb with orange rays shooting out shafts of light to illuminate treetops and bathe the glistening moors in a pink haze. Before long it drops over the horizon and my reverie is over. Ralph has left early, thank goodness, and the sound of departing cars indicates that 5:00 p.m. has passed and the factory hands are going home. The machinery has been switched off - soon the surrounding moor will reclaim this last corner and gather it up into the night silence.

Twilight sinks into darkness and I search Ralph's desk for his gold pen. Then, locking up the office, I collect my car and drive the short distance to the river bank parking neatly behind the peat mountain. It is not long before the factory lights are all extinguished and the last car has driven away. Outside there is a soft east wind, speaking of better weather to come perhaps. A heron reluctantly flies away from the riverbank where it has been waiting, motionless, for signs of a fish supper. His ungainly body and drooping legs remind one of a pterodactyl, perhaps one of the few remaining vestiges of original moorland life. The river laps contentedly, the breeze rustles the reeds and I mark the quarters of my proposed circle with the aid of a compass. Groping in the dark I fill a bowl with river water and another with peat and place them west and north. Two swan's feathers mark the east and, with some trepidation, I light the hurricane lamp to mark the south - now there is evidence of my presence should anyone be in the vicinity. Finally I take the pen and lay it in the centre with the communion bread and wine.

Gathering myself together I mentally surround myself with a gold light and fix my mind on the job in hand, excluding the outside world with as much discipline as I can muster. With my athame I slowly and methodically cast a circle around me. Focusing intently I summon the elements in turn and then in a hushed voice call upon the Lady and Lord to witness this rite. After a suitable pause I state my case and ask for peace to prevail when the pen is used, offering it up for inspection at the four quarters as 'exhibit A' . I am following my instincts entirely now. The old hurricane lamp has blown out so, although the circle is less conspicuous, I feel a little amateurish in my performance and trust in the Gods' good nature. Concentrating heavily on peace and directing this thought around the circle and into the pen, now returned to the centre, I reach for bread and wine already beginning to feel quite spaced out. My nervousness has left me and as I lift the wine glass to toast the Lord and Lady I am filled with a sense of well being and growing enchantment. The full moon is slowly rising, dignified and gracious - I pause in admiration and savour the moment, the temporal world is a long way away. For an indeterminate length of time I stand transfixed, lost in the wonder of some unfamiliar dimension, suspended between heaven and earth quite unconscious of my surroundings. One sip of wine has not provoked this effect, this is a magical sensation.

Time to close the circle and depart. With thanks I salute the quarters and bid farewell to the Lady and Lord. Rather sadly I gather up my tools, emptying the water and peat into the centre of the circle which will now be left to fade overnight. Unobserved I load the car and drive home, tomorrow I will return the pen. Whatever may come of this I have had a magic moment, a mystical union when moon and sky, heart and soul, merged into one and I rose above the mundane for a brief interval. For this I am thankful.

....

Mild and misty at sunrise. Later I watch the full moon rise over 'my little cabin built of clay', so isolated and shrouded by trees, skeleton fingers clasp the outer walls, cobwebs of black shadow lie on the moonlit road and I dance amongst them, happy to be alone under the night sky.

....

A true spring day. Pale sunshine is throwing a haze on the tree trunks. In the meadow behind the cottage the herd of Friesians are grazing, out for the first time this year. They frisk and butt one another, full of the joys of Spring. After lunch I plant an apple tree in the garden - a gift to the Goddess, She who holds apples sacred - and a thing of beauty for me to watch as it matures.

....

It is Oestre (Easter to the Christians). Now the sap starts to rise in plant and Man and what is termed nowadays as the 'Growing Season' begins in earnest. All winter I have kept my lawn trimmed so I don't have to plough through shaggy tufts of grass but everything now starts to spurt, weeds as well as flowers. In seven weeks the growth rate will slow down and it will be White Sunday (Whitsun to the Christians), the day to remember the Goddess who will bless the world with white blossom on tree and hedgerow.

Solitude

Lingering thoughts as dusk returns to night
A tardy blackbird makes his homeward flight
Again I watch a day draw to its' close
Thanking God for solitude and repose.
Behind me lies the clamour of the herd
No longer do I yearn to join their world
The vain temptations urging mankind on
Visit me no more - their power has gone.
Perhaps a wistful moment here and there
But no, the freedom gained cannot compare.

To see, to watch, to savour all Creation
Unhampered by the cares that rule the nation
To surrender time and yet to gain eternity
Then sacrifice yourself into infinity
Only those who take the road unsigned
Will know and understand the great design
And then the role that each agreed to play
Will be revealed to all who choose this way
The promise made before you first drew breath
Remembering those who'll greet you on your death.

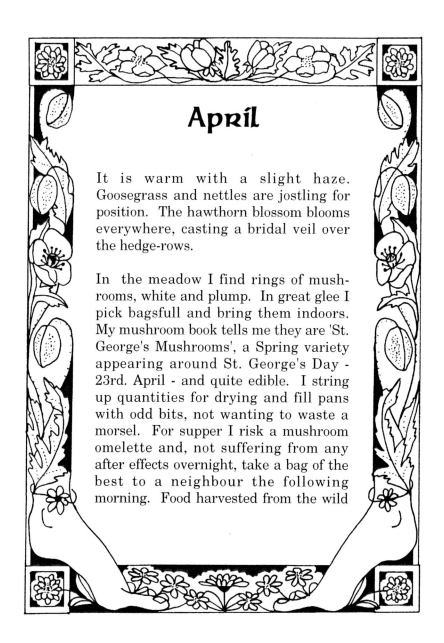

April

It is warm with a slight haze. Goosegrass and nettles are jostling for position. The hawthorn blossom blooms everywhere, casting a bridal veil over the hedge-rows.

In the meadow I find rings of mushrooms, white and plump. In great glee I pick bagsfull and bring them indoors. My mushroom book tells me they are 'St. George's Mushrooms', a Spring variety appearing around St. George's Day - 23rd. April - and quite edible. I string up quantities for drying and fill pans with odd bits, not wanting to waste a morsel. For supper I risk a mushroom omelette and, not suffering from any after effects overnight, take a bag of the best to a neighbour the following morning. Food harvested from the wild

is a pleasure that is hard to beat, something those who trundle monotonously round Sainsburys will never know.

....

We awake to snow this morning, slushy underfoot and bitterly cold. Later in the day it comes down more steadily, blanketing rooftops and hillsides. Now, this evening the landscape is shining clean and the late evening sunrays gild the meadow, every droplet a prism. In the distance the hills are white and wintry but down on the flatlands it is Spring again.

....

More snow today, lying for an hour or two on the ground, followed by fierce hail.

....

Once more the moon has waxed to the full and the nights are becoming more mild. Nearby is an ancient 'Faerie Fort', a low hill which is still rough pasture and strewn with wild flowers. It stands, brooding over the surrounding countryside, which is composed of gentle hills, woods and flatlands stretching out to the western coastline. At its foot is a small unspoiled village; church and manor, farmyard and cot all having a somewhat medieval air about them. Little is known about Lullup Hill outside the pagan community, consequently it is unfrequented and the Trig Point which graces its crest and makes an excellent altar, when seen from below, reminds one of a burial cairn of some long dead chieftain entombed in the hill.

I decide to view the Lady from these heights and possibly perform a suitable ceremony. Throughout the winter the power of the moon has influenced me considerably, I am always drawn to offer some small act of worship when she glides gracefully into view, fully present and beaming down on us all. Certainly it can be a tense time for everyone but always my primitive urges are stirred and on Lullup Hill I trust that I can find the privacy and inspiration to commune in some personal way with our Mother.

After dark I drive to Combeley, the village lying so snugly underneath the fold of hills which rises from the flood plain out of the sea. Parking the car I make my way up a back lane and down a bridle path which leads to the foot of the Fort. It is still thickly muddied at this time of year but I am well equipped and plod methodically on gathering a small posy of wild flowers on the way. Ahead is a stile and I clamber over, slipping and sliding, to face Lullup Hill itself, smoothly rounded, illuminated in the moonlight; to my right is a belt of dark unkempt woodland and all around is silence, the silence of an undisturbed wilderness, the deep hush of a place unexploited by Man. Half expecting to be accosted by Presences of some kind I laboriously scale the hill and arrive at the Trig. Point breathless, but instantly enchanted by the view. I place my small floral offering on this ready made 'altar' and survey the scene more fully. To the west is the sea coast, framed by sloping hills, the flat levels neatly cut into squares of pasture intersected by straight cut waterways. The geometry is occasionally broken up by meandering rivers and flooded tracts, evidence of the remains of the Cleansing Tide recently passed. All is typical of the west - water in all its forms, its insidious, churning power, relentlessly and silently re-shaping the soul of the land.

To the north are hills; Abbeybridge Knoll in the distance, a clear star-studded sky and the sense of a vast, and endless landmass beyond. In the east are woodlands, crowned by the rising moon, magical and undiscovered, containing who knows what? Turning to the south I find ancient hills slipping into flat plains, the lights of one or two villages cluster bravely together but over all a blanket of soft darkness.

I survey the scene, drinking it in by the light of the moon, quite alone and unthreatened by interruptions. This is a friendly place, a centre, a focus. It is not difficult to see the hand of God in the landscape, sculpturing and shaping the world. The Lady beams down in approval, offering sheen and shadows where Her ghostly fingers touch hilltops and valleys, water courses and woodland.

Time slows down and I pace out a circle, calling on the spirits of the four elements to attend me, pausing at each quarter to raise my arms and give full voice to my request, quite uninhibited as a result of my solitary state. In the centre, at the Trig. Point I call upon the Lady, the Mother, Mistress of the Moon to shine down and bless me in my magic circle. This concentrated effort focuses my attention on the veil that separates the worlds and I feel it thin slightly as I turn my gaze to the moon, sailing proudly and gloriously across the night sky. I am uplifted by the sight and my inner spirit reaches upwards in an attempt to bridge the gap between earth and sky; so utterly beautiful are my surroundings, so charged with ancient power - the air full of whisperings. I am quite alone with the Goddess above me and Faerie enchantment echoing around the hills and valleys at my feet. This is what I have surrendered my worldly ways for, this moment of communion, inexplicable, captivating and totally absorbing. I truly feel at one with all of nature, everything the mystics over the centuries have attempted to explain is now mine and, as with those who have gone before, I am lost for words, ensnared in a web of wonder and delight.

I sit for some time in meditation and offer a prayer for mankind, for those multitudes who have not discovered the hidden path, the mystic way. Then, rising reluctantly, I retrace my steps around the circle and give my thanks to the elemental spirits for keeping watch. Finally I offer my gratitude to the Lady and, bowing deeply to the moon, rather sadly weave my way downhill to the stile and the muddy path that leads to the village. In the gloaming a deer wafts past me and disappears into the woods.

No sooner do I find myself on level ground than a feeling of tremendous buoyancy arises within me, something I haven't felt for many long years. My spirits soar and I am filled with a dancing beat, lightly tripping along through the puddles, springing from turf to tuft, sprightly under the moonlight. There is a sense of happiness around me as if I am in the midst of a joyful company; this is indeed Faerie, I am being attended by the spirits of Lullup Hill, escorted safely back. A blessing indeed.

Soon the lane narrows and turns sharply downward to the village. I feel my invisible escort departing and finish the journey alone, my spirits as flat as before. The car is waiting where I left it and, as I struggle with muddy wellingtons, take one last look up at the moon and the shadowy hill lying in the distance. Just a dream, just an interlude, a fantasy perhaps. Whatever it was I shall return next month and once more seek communion with She who graces the night sky and those who still protect their ancient hill and welcome worshippers of the Old Religion.

....

Baby rabbits scamper through the wild marguerites. Embryonic cow parsley unfurls along the roadside, skeleton willows display pale green lacy shawls. At night the sky is clear and I lean over the garden gate watching the whirling star patterns, observing the Pleiades low down on the western horizon. In a week or two they will disappear completely, then it will be 'summer' by the old ways, and we shall be under the domain of the Goddess.

....

Today the sun crosses the equator into the northern hemisphere and we can at last look forward to some long-denied warmth. The swallows have returned from their winter quarters and dot the telegraph wires, their blue and black plumage glowing iridescent in the sun. They are such attractive birds, their contours so sharply defined, their movements so graceful as they swoop and soar, catching their food on the wing.

....

Chartreuse fields of indeterminate corn glisten, water-coloured in the warm sun, gently swaying in the breeze. Wild garlic on the roadside is heavily molested by flies. Late blooming trees stand like charcoal sticks, stark and defiantly basic, uncloaked, uncamoflauged, remaining sentinels of winter, casting a short shadow. It is a hesitant time of year - 'You go first' they tell the willows who, lacking such a firm foundation, are happy to don their party clothes. Still there are banks of cowslips on the roadside now joined by clouds of pale pink lady's smock. I note that the rooks are nesting very low this year - the sign of a poor summer ahead.

Such splendour requires closer inspection and, during a break in the showers when hot sunshine spreads across the land I stroll up the lane and branch off up a track which leads to a lonely cottage and some panoramic views of the surrounding countryside. It is a slow climb and I linger along the wayside admiring the rich vegetation and drinking in the fragrances and sensations of the season. So much changes so quickly at this time of year one must grasp at the moment, savouring the awakening of flower and shrub, the unfurling leaf, the pale translucent colours which will quickly deepen with maturity and the delicate bloom, so short lived, soon to drop its petals for another year.

Somewhat out of breath I reach the cottage, standing alone amidst the cornfields, stone walls braced to take the brunt of the hilltop winds. Nearby is a thorn tree, an attractive specimen, fully grown to about twenty foot with evenly spaced branches supported by a slightly twisted trunk. The thorns that are so apparent in winter are now obscured by bursting buds but still, silhouetted against the sky, dark brown and solitary, it is a fine example of the Faerie tree as the thorn has always been known.

I sit down thankfully underneath it, leaning against the weathered trunk, brushed by prickly branches. There is a hint of white in the ripening buds and a delicious green tinge to the unfurling leaves, so damp and fragile like all newborn things. In days past new hawthorn leaves were eaten as a salad - 'bread and cheese' it was called for some unknown reason. I look up to the higher branches and muse on the tree as a whole, the masculine thorniness and weather-beaten boughs now touched with a feminine softness of white and green as the Goddess emerges from within, sap rising and mingling with natural forces to produce a harmonious balance of gender.

Whimsically I mutter to the tree 'You're a very fine thorn tree, I must say'. Unbelievably, from somewhere deep within the trunk, comes a weary voice. 'I'll be a great deal finer when these leaves unfurl'.

Astonished, I abruptly turn round, thinking that someone is teasing me, but there is no one there. It was the thorn tree that spoke, there is no doubt about that. I realize that the voice was heard by my inner senses and gaze in wonder, waiting for further comments. But no, nothing more is heard and as I stare in disbelief at the tree I realize that it is bowed down with curled leaves; indeed in a few days when they unclasp and are able to be supported by the breeze a tremendous weight will be lifted off the branches. I am dumbfounded by my discovery - to speak to trees and growing things is quite a customary practice of mine and of all witches, but to receive an answer as I have done, spoken in a rather stern and matter of fact way, is a new experience. Shocked, I stare in admiration at this dear old thorn, so weighted down with burgeoning life, so patiently waiting for its leaves to fully develop so that it too can sway lightly in the wind, carefree and unburdened. I pat its trunk warmly and whisper 'soon, soon' then walk meditatively back down the lane, pausing at the turning for one last look at the thorn, resolutely supporting its burden, contributing to the surge of new life that pulses amongst hill and dale alike. Smiling, hugging my new secret, I skip childishly back down the hill.

....

Beltane: I rise in the dark to climb the Knoll. The sky is showing first light as I park the car, it is cold but the air is clear and worthy of some deep breaths. As I climb through the early morning mist, the grass sodden beneath my boots, I am aware of an enchanted world below me. Like an underwater scene, trees and flat fields lie, mistily shrouded, unreal, swimming in a vast inland sea. At some point I break through the 'veil' to find, by now, shooting rays of bright sunshine and distant hilltops emerging like islands from a thick bed of opaque white mist. It is even more of a 'sea scene'; all is fluid and floating as white vapour swirls below me, above a dazzling blue sky and the shining green turf of the Knoll, colour-washed in the early Spring sunshine. To be alive this morning is pure joy, to be alive and active enough to climb the Knoll at sunrise, is an achievement treasured only by those who have previously been denied this pleasure. Halfway up I pause to catch my breath and, as I gaze at the surrounding landscape, slowly turning to embrace each clinging droplet, every piercing sunbeam, I am moved to tears at the exquisite beauty of this moment. Although I am alone the air is not hushed, there is a joyful expectancy, a new beginning. Today, Beltane, is the first day of summer and the Goddess has set out Her glittering stall for the world to see. After the inertia of winter and the hesitancy of early Spring, Life is everywhere, glowing in the dawn sky, pulsing through the Knoll, thrumming through my body and charging my spirits which arise in a rush of ecstasy; I am inordinately thankful to be here at this time, experiencing the wonder of re-creation. Too moved to form words in my mind I trust that the Goddess understands my feelings and climb onward to the crest of the Knoll. Here I survey the entire panorama, now gilded by full sunshine, the mist dispersing before my very eyes revealing an all too solid outlook, less magical and shrouded than a few minutes earlier, the familiar Somerset Levels - waterways and willows.

A group of bedraggled early risers roam across the crest of the Knoll, also glad to greet the sunrise this Beltane. The local Druid Grove is organising a circle, Morris Men wait in the wings and one or two cloaked female figures whirl through the Tower, the final remains of a ruined church. It is bitterly cold but, undaunted, everyone circles and chants, watching the eastern horizon out of the corner of their eye. The Spring Maiden, who must be well over 45. is 'wheeled' into the circle, she is lavishly dressed in velvet robes and gold jewellry but is as gauche as a teenager. When invited to invoke the elements she stumbles over her words, runs dry and is assisted by the senior Druid whose loud tones echo round the circle. He faces east, blows his long horn and the sun obligingly comes fully into view. There is no pause of acknowledgment, no moment of awe, the Morris Dancers bound into sight, jumping about furiously to keep warm. Someone has lit a small fire and I warm myself beside it, drinking coffee from a thermos; the 'witches' no longer whirl, they are wrapped up tightly in their cloaks, frozen to the marrow.

I stand in solitary contemplation overlooking the slopes of the Knoll trying to recapture the enchantment of that incipient moment so recently passed. Alas, all is now sunny splendour and human life joins the life of the earth, surging forward in celebration of the returning summer and it's anticipated fruitfulness. I wander away, slowly wending my way down the hillside, back to the car.

A Beltane hint: To Call a Lover

When the moon is waxing in Taurus or Libra take three pinches of Dragons' Blood and drop them on either burning coals or charcoal, calling your lover's name each time. S/he should appear in 24 hours.

Knee High on Mellis Common

A brazen daisy dips and sways
A poppy nods her head
The golden smile of buttercup guile
Defies a wintry bed.

A creamy carpet crimson flecked
Triumphant after sleep
A joyful throng of thrusting song
A bower cradle deep.

Now Mellis Common comes to life
And scorns her withered weeds
Springs' starry cloak in me invokes
A wild and urgent need.

So take my clogs, my worn out boots
And leave me naked feet
Take petticoats and muffled throats
I hear a dancing beat.

Knee high splendour lush and cool
With whispering, stroking grasp
Fulfils my soul, my limbs enfold
Succumbed to nature's clasp.

Before my eyes a sweeping sea
A fragile drifting pool.
Bless petalled stooks and beckoning looks
For lifting winter's rule.

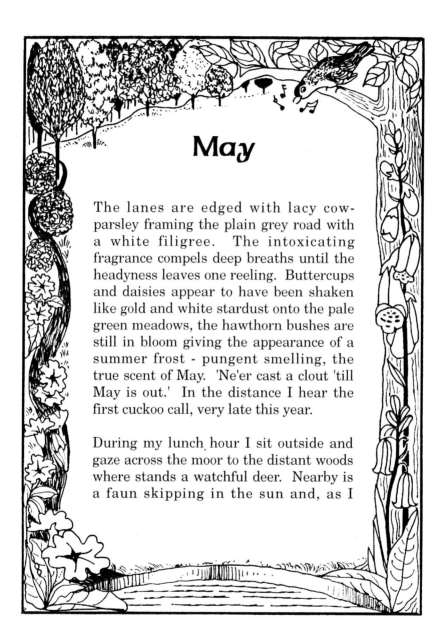

May

The lanes are edged with lacy cow-parsley framing the plain grey road with a white filigree. The intoxicating fragrance compels deep breaths until the headyness leaves one reeling. Buttercups and daisies appear to have been shaken like gold and white stardust onto the pale green meadows, the hawthorn bushes are still in bloom giving the appearance of a summer frost - pungent smelling, the true scent of May. 'Ne'er cast a clout 'till May is out.' In the distance I hear the first cuckoo call, very late this year.

During my lunch hour I sit outside and gaze across the moor to the distant woods where stands a watchful deer. Nearby is a faun skipping in the sun and, as I

follow her gaze I see another, it's twin, galloping along one of the many ditches dug for peat excavation. No wonder she is exposing herself to public gaze, her offspring is trapped, too weak to climb out of the channel, running backwards and forwards in distress. I attract the attention of one of the factory hands, a countryman who has lived here all his life and he obligingly sets out across the moor, although all too slowly for my liking. He is unable to assist but mercifully two others join in the rescue mission and the faun is lifted out and sent off back to mother who retreats back into the woods with her family. As I watch distractedly I am suddenly struck by the fact that our office has recently become a more peaceful place and Ralph's tantrums have been reduced to mere irritability. This hits me like a thunderbolt and I stop in my tracks, stunned by the realisation. The spellworking has had an effect, my plea was heard, I am not such an amateur after all. I send out thanks into the ether.

....

A calm Spring day followed by an equally calm, clear evening sends me down to the river after work to inspect my boat and reconnect with the spirits of the west, the water sprites. I stand on the plank bridge drinking in the view of the now glistening moor, dappled by sunlight and shadows and turning from brown to bright green as the sap rises. The river bank is a vivid yellow, thickly edged with rape, rogue seeds spread on the wind. Water rats gliding out from their winter retreats somersault in mid-stream sending ripples along the rhyne which stretches straight and true before and behind me. Newly hatched ducklings zigzag uncertainly after their careless mothers, speculative gnats hover on the surface of the water. There is speedwell in the grass and cuckoos calling in the distance. It is all too tempting and, full of sudden euphoria at nature's bounty, I don my wellingtons and strip the tarpaulin off the boat. The paint is flaking off but there has been no major damage from the winter weather and, scrambling through the thigh-high nettles, I soon have it launched and climb aboard.

I had forgotten how therapeutic it is to sail gently downstream. Only slight rustles in the grass and the lapping of the water disturb the peace. In the deep golden light of early evening the rape is luminescent, standing tall; a shelter between the narrow river and the wide moorland. It is reflected in the rippling water and I row down a yellow colonnade towards the western sunset, noting with pleasure that the willow, so brutally hacked down last year, has returned to life and sent out many long shoots which will soon restore its' graceful figure. Behind it the 'faerie thorn' remains untouched, the guardian of the river I always feel.

Lazily drifting and dreaming, I round the bend in the river and can see the outline of the Knoll lying in the early evening mist. There is so much beauty here, such vastness above and below that one feels one's spirit expanding in sympathy. The complete solitude and natural tranquillity calms my soul and the fresh colours feed my senses, dulled by the drabness of winter. I row a little more fiercely to make some headway against the changing current and note the landmarks which are mercifully unchanged since last year: the narrow culvert, the three large willows in a row, a deserted swan's nest. Soon they will be breeding again and lines of cygnets will glide downstream in the wake of their parents. For now I am glad to see that all is in order and no intruders have spoilt this small stretch of paradise where I am able to re-connect with Goddess and God, away from human violation. Sighing in rapture I turn the boat round and face the sinking sun. It is time to go back - just a short trip this time, not to be spoilt by the gathering dusk nor the chill of evening. I raise the oars and allow the boat to go with the flow, finding its own way back through eddies and whirls and small cross currents. Water is being pumped off the land back into the rhyne and as we pass the boat catches in the fast channel created by this influx and we are carried quickly back to the plank bridge. I grasp at the vegetation on the bank and pull up, climbing out and tugging the boat up after me. This is always a difficult feat - a heavy load, a slippery rope and a sharp incline. However, I have found that, in the absence of muscle a certain amount of mental effort helps and I heave the boat mercilessly onto dry land thinking fiercely of an ex lover who brutally jilted many years ago. My retrospective anger does the trick and 'Undine' is well and truly beached.

I make the necessary fastenings and pause for a final moment of appreciation. There is great poignancy in the scene as long shadows break across the moor and the deep orange sun sinks all too rapidly below the horizon. Soon the night creatures will venture forth and the water birds will hide under the reeds for the night. In the distance the Knoll is already black and the woods behind me loom menacingly where only a short time ago they beckoned a green welcome. I sigh with a mixture of satisfaction and sorrow - a winter has passed and the rhyne is still flowing, my boat is unharmed and ahead lies a summer of pleasant evenings on the water. But all is transient, in life we are in death, in sunshine there is shadow, in light there is darkness; spring will give way to summer and then there will be autumn and another winter. With the mixed emotions that these realisations bring I turn for home, a final glance at the landscape now smiling sleepily. There is much to look forward to.

....

I have not forgotten my original plan to re-connect with the elements. At this time of year the Firewalk comes to town, run by a strong minded woman who has trained with the Native American Indians.

The Firewalk is practiced by many primitive cultures and is considered to be a test of spiritual strength for the participants, enabling them to use the principle of mind over matter to reach unprecedented heights of awareness. Originally it was a male preserve, women being expected to break through all necessary pain barriers during childbirth. Nowadays the Firewalk is available to everyone and travelling 'facilitators' replicate the traditional ceremony for the surprisingly large number of people who apply to walk barefoot over a bed of coals in order to either approach or achieve a state of near ecstasy.

I part with a tidy sum of money and book my place at a location to be announced nearer the time not knowing quite what to expect but trusting that the Goddess will uphold me if the need arises.

I am no stranger to the element of fire and hold it in high esteem. Its consuming powers and lively energies are a wonder and a delight. Whilst I am incapable of igniting a fire through friction I flatter myself that I can manage both indoor and outdoor fires to my satisfaction and find great solace in contemplating both flame and ember, spark and inferno. Great indeed is the salamander, now I am going to test my powers against his.

....

Goosegrass pulls at my clothes as I wander the high-banked lanes drinking in the warmth and security that is offered. Low-flying blackbirds, intent on business and noisy starlings with indignant voices, fill the air. After dark I stand at the garden gate listening to the nightingales singing in the distant trees.

....

The meadow beyond the gate has been left for hay this year and is already thigh high in buttercups. The sorrel has also emerged and has added a contrasting texture to the otherwise grey-green mixture of grasses that thicken and grow before our very eyes. As the buttercups bloom and quickly disperse so the red and white clover takes their place looking sturdier but far less glamourous. Still the delicate cow parsley fills the corner of the meadow, lacy, towering high now, a touch of feminine charm added to a rather masculine landscape. The trees, all now in full leaf, stand like galleons amidst a sea of waving grass, each a noble being, individual, sturdy, wrapped in summer splendour.

My small garden is also a picture of fertility, much is foliage at present but here and there a bloom shows its' head. All the neighbourhood snails have been congregating here and making many meals out of my carefully cultivated plants. Each one bears evidence of a midnight feast and two weeks ago I decided to do some reclaiming. Consequently I hunted the snails down and threw them far into the meadow whereupon the garden began to recover. This afternoon whilst idly contemplating this renewed fertility I glance down at the base of the fence and see an army of snails approaching from the meadow....hundreds of them - well, perhaps fifty or so. All are active, some have begun to scale the fence, others are bunched in groups with a single advanced guard leading them onwards towards the Elysian Fields of my garden. At the rear more snails are splayed out, travelling resolutely towards the main body from all directions. Every snail I have evicted appears to be here, I am being assaulted in true army fashion, bombarded by my enemies. There is clearly some sort of unity and method in their manoeuvres and I am more than impressed; in fact a little daunted at this illustration of cogent thought which has produced such a unified onslaught. Much strategic planning must have gone into this, much shared resentment and animosity must have provoked such organised retaliation.

I watch, fascinated by their efforts; the bravado of the front line, the determination of the ranks and the enthusiasm of the rearguard. Sadly the attempt failed after about half an hour. A few brave souls made it over the top but the rest turned around and trundled off back into the meadow - a defeated army; perhaps some sense of my presence undermined their resolve. I hurl the successful invaders back into the meadow, no doubt they returned home heroes - or heroines perhaps.

....

The days are lengthening and the bright clear blue skies entice one further out of doors. Light breezes play across the meadow, ruffling rich green grass, and flowers are dappled by light and shade, nodding and smiling in the sun, blooming in their fullness.

Again I lean over the garden gate breathing in the freshness of the day, longing to encapsulate it somehow, to be brought out again at mid-winter. I lift my face to the sky, drinking in the long forgotten radiance of the sun, full of a sense of well-being. Every morning when I stand in the garden and raise my arms in greeting to 'The Sun, the Giver of Life' I long for this time of year. Somewhere behind the grey winter skies the fire is still burning; sad little winter dawns offer no more than a low, red glow but it is enough to know that we are not entirely abandoned and that the crimson arc will one day blaze in full glory out of a summer sky. I watch its' movement from Capricorn to Cancer, each day getting stronger and rising higher. Then a pause at the zenith and the slow mellow journey back to Capricorn. Alone, barely awake, clad in my dressing gown in winter but naked in summer, I reach for the sky, for light and life, renewal and the strength to face a new day.

....

Now I bask in the early summer sunshine, offering my body up for a blessing, soaking up the heat and allowing my eyes to roam along the distant horizon. Graceful dancing willows in the foreground speak of unseen dikes and runnels. Beyond, my eye is caught by the deep green of the woods, rounded and full with summer foliage. I sense their cool shady places, the lacy canopy of bough and blade, the stirring of the leaf mold underfoot as woodland animals emerge from winter hibernation. It is time to seek the Lord and Lady in their sacred setting, to find a space of my own within the wildwood.

I am not long in finding my way across the moors to my destination. A winding country lane runs between the trees and I park discreetly under the spreading branches of a beech. Here I enter another world, hushed and full of hidden mystery. I am undoubtedly an interloper and a stranger and I tread warily through the thicket, alert and watchful. Untouched woodland never fails to enchant the trespasser, it has a life of its own, timeless and intensely private. Although home to well-known animals and birds, there is more than that - a web of wonder has been spun around it or a binding spell, encasing and protecting, weaving together trees and undergrowth, flora and fauna, into a tight unit. Overseeing all this is Faerie, the Spirits of the Undead, watching over the Dryads stretching their lordly arms upward to the sky and outward to touch and mingle with neighbouring trees, protecting and encouraging young shoots as they thrust their way out of the thick layer of fallen leaves which has been their winter bedding.

Moving beyond the rough wilderness of the perimeter where bramble and honeysuckle entwine and ensnare I reach a glade of birches, white flaking bark, straight, even trunks. The topmost branches sigh in the breeze and everywhere is a mild creaking and groaning. Underfoot is a sea of bluebells, the unique blue tinge of the flowers and shining green leaves looking lusciously inviting. I long to run barefoot across them, to stretch out on my back and savour the heavenly smell; instead I pick a small bunch and seek out the narrow trackway that leads deeper into the wood.

Now I step warily, avoiding dry sticks that crack and disturb the deep silence of the heart of the woods. Sunrays pierce the shadowy canopy of leaves, illuminating cuckoo pint and bluebell, woodbine and late celandine. All around is the sighing of boughs, the trilling of birds and a sensation of watchfulness, of being observed, of unseen presences large and small, hovering in hidden places. I stop abruptly and establish my bearings. This is a planted woodland, glade upon glade of deciduous trees, mature and well rooted, tempered and toughened by the passing seasons. Ivy clings to their trunks and throws out tendrils, catching and curling around newer saplings. Hazel wands sprout between the trees, stunted, eternal shrubs with flat, perfectly formed leaves showing translucent in the sunbeams.

There is a lot to absorb and I feel my chakras opening in wonder, grasping at the essence of this enchanted place, offering myself up as an integral part of breeze and branch, flower and fold. Lightly I move on and in front of me, quick and agile, runs a deer. She is gone before I can blink, her dappled brown body melding with the background shadows. Not a sound has she made, a shy wild creature, watchful and vulnerable, even in her native habitat.

The trees thin out and I am facing a field of sprouting maze. To my right is a small stream running over rocks and disappearing into a hidden ditch. I cross over, stepping gingerly on the stones, and find more woodland - a narrow path leading into dense undergrowth. Clearly no one has trodden this way for some time and I am soon enshrouded by greenery. Up ahead is a large oak tree, the area around its' base smooth and clear of debris; it is a giant of the woods, spreading its sturdy branches benevolently over the surrounding scrub. Lobed leaves, spring green and newly unfurled dance and flutter, dressing their mighty host with chartreuse splendour. I gaze upward in awe, still now, soothed by my ramblings.

Faeries and witches are the remnants of a race of people who believed that everything had spirits - tree, stone, mineral etc. Once upon a time everyone believed this but sometime, long, long ago, a group of Irish monks did a very successful conversion job on the populace and managed to convince them that this was not so. Consequently their qualms about slashing and burning, quarrying and mining were subdued and agriculture was born which gave rise to better quality food and an end to the nomadic tradition. The rest is history and has led up to the modern disregard for Mother Nature and her beneficence which will shortly be thoroughly depleted. So, in true witch fashion, I try to connect with the spirit of the tree, tuning in to its' vibrations as best I can, showing respect for its' tenacity in a hostile world.

At the foot of the oak is a hollow and, by nestling carefully within its folds I can rest securely with my face turned sunward. Here is peace and submission to nature - I can feel myself blending with creation, sinking back against the tree, my brain slowing down and a sleepy peace stealing over me - back in the arms of the Mother.

After a period of time, as the sun moves gently out of my vision, I stir from my reverie and look around. There is no evidence of human habitation here, no litter nor damage; wood pigeons flutter and coo and branches creak, but I am clearly the only visitor who has been here for some time.

It occurs to me that this is an ideal setting for an outdoor circle - a mighty oak and a bubbling stream, privacy and peace. There is sufficient bare ground under the tree to allow for a five foot circle and I clear the remains of roots and weeds in anticipation of this, pleased with the effect and anxious to bring it into being.

Fired with enthusiasm I head back to the car, planning to return at a later date with some equipment. I take another trail, overgrown and restricted by long creepers which catch at my ankles and more hazel wands which snick my face. There is still a feeling of presences, benign, mildly interested in me but welcoming enough; I feel I can return here at any time.

The bluebells have wilted in my hand but are revived at home by a drink of water.

....

I have visited the oak tree frequently over the last few days. Today I bring a compass which helps me find the directions and trace an outline of salt to delineate the circle, marking the quarters with stones. I need a stang. An ash stang to act as an altar. Casting round in my mind for a mental picture of the ash tree I scan the woods for something that looks likely. Alas, my school nature walks have been in vain, I cannot summon an ash tree, not even an ash leaf. Disappointed in my inadequacies I feel I've drawn a blank and cannot continue with this. Nevertheless I cast the circle, using an imaginary green light, and sit within, meditating deeply, hoping that the Faerie Queen will approve of my creation.

On my way home, passing through a double line of trees, which sway and toss in the early evening breeze I hear a rustling in the fallen leaves and stop abruptly. There, to my delight, is a baby badger, tumbling and capering over the ground. As I stand motionless, fully expecting my presence to cause alarm, I see it is joined by another and the two of them race down a shallow incline, grunting happily. Then a third joins them from a distance and there is a trio frolicking together in the last slanting sunrays, quite unaware of my observations, jumping amongst the fallen leaves, nuzzling and tumbling downhill where, one by one, they disappear underground.

I linger for a moment or two but they do not make a re-appearance and, as there are no other signs of life, I move on, pleased to have witnessed such an unexpected scene and feeling a greater part of the wildwood.

....

This evening I join a group of prospective firewalkers at a nearby private house, lent for the occasion; most people appear a little nervous and unsure of quite what to expect. We are given a warm welcome by Eliza, our hostess and facilitator who, with bleached blonde hair and wide smile, gives us a short, introductory talk on the background of the Firewalk. Her enthusiasm is infectious and we are soon trekking outside to watch one or two men lighting the fire according to the ancient ritual practice in order to achieve the correct temperature and constituency for the embers.

Our walk will not take place for an hour or two so, whilst we await both nightfall and sinking coals, we socialise back indoors and listen to Eliza who has us enthralled by her Firewalk experiences and manages to whip us all up to a fever pitch of anticipation. To her eternal credit she answers the unspoken question 'What happens if we fail?'

There is silence in the room as she catalogues past failures and explains the reason. All is sympathy for the nervous, for those of us who try but do not succeed, and encouragement to make another attempt in future. One or two previous failures amongst us speak up, they are back for a re-try and we are sustained by their fallibility.

Eliza carefully explains the logistics of the operation, we are to file outside barefoot, slowly circle the bed of coals, whilst chanting an Indian chant. This will no doubt set up a suitable atmosphere, allowing for a sense of unity and a calm mindful approach. As individuals find themselves in front of the firebed so they will be at liberty to peel off from the circle and walk across, dowsing their feet at the end in a trough of water. In this way everyone has many chances 'to walk' as the circle continues to revolve, so if courage arises slowly or strikes one with a lightning flash then there will be no shortage of opportunities. Everyone appears to be satisfied with this arrangement but as I glance round at the thirty or so people who are 'to walk' tonight I sense acute tension manifesting in a mounting excitement where laughter may quickly give way to tears.

'You will ask yourself what the hell you are doing here' says Eliza, 'and - if my mother could see me now! This is not Saturday night at the cinema, the Firewalk is an ancient mystical rite - a spiritual ordeal.' She smiles winningly, sensing our misgivings. We collectively gulp and glance across at the exit. In the following pause, before we have a chance to throw in the towel, Eliza musters us all into a tight standing group. We are obliged to sing a brief four-line song about triumph which sticks in my throat, I just want to get on with it. Then we file outside.

The night is black dark, stars proclaim a clear sky but it is cool and the grass beneath our feet is wringing wet. Now quite eager to proceed we form a circle, obediently chanting, and view the Firewalk from the corner of our eyes. The earlier bonfire has disintegrated, leaving red hot remains, bright in the darkness, still sending up small licking flames. The two male assistants rake them out into an oblong shape and the flames are quenched, coals and cinders lie in a deep glowing bed, a crimson patch in the darkness. On these we are expected to walk, some perhaps even dance across, as

Eliza has gleefully told us, does happen. 'I must be barking mad' I think to myself, her words coming back to me, and then, right on cue, 'If my mother could see me now!'

Round and round we circle, chanting, absorbed in our private thoughts which are no doubt all following on along the same lines. Privacy has been guaranteed and, funnily enough, that is the most comforting thought of all. There will be no judgment, no post mortems, no excuses needed for success or failure, this is a very personal event, one to strengthen the spirit, our own innermost soul.

After a few circuits my feet are so icy cold I can barely feel them. The stars are glowing more brightly now and, as I gaze up at them, I consider the many young Indian braves who have performed the Firewalk under starlit skies over the centuries. We have been promised elation or even euphoria afterwards but I take a pragmatic stance, autosuggestion is a powerful force.

Two women station themselves either side of the walk to assist us if necessary and catch us if we fall. The trough of water is placed at the far end of the coals and one of the men stands in position, hose in hand, while the other faces him in a businesslike fashion. This is it then, there is no escape. I wonder if I have really over-reached myself at last.

Still we circle and chant, it is getting a little tedious now. The heat from the fire is enough to keep us fairly warm but my feet are numb. Suddenly Eliza announces that we are now free to 'walk' but there is no response, we are locked into a circuit, summoning our courage, each privately dreading the moment when we might make enormous fools of ourselves, beaten into submission by the God of Fire. Everyone is waiting for someone else to make the first move.

Then, in one quick movement, Eliza peels off and marches confidently across the coals beaming, her yellow hair and white garments showing clearly in the darkness. Four smart paces and she is across, feet in the trough, supported by the two men and then moving on back into the circle. 'Of course Eliza has done this hundreds of times' we are thinking. But no - there goes another, running across the coals, and then another and a third. It is quick, there is no hesitation at the brink, one marches across and as she reaches the trough, so she is pursued by running feet and she in turn makes way for others. People are peeling off right, left and centre, I'll never get a turn at this rate - now I'm eager to face the fire, to trip lightly across as the others have done. I pace the circle, if no one beats me to it I'll walk next time round, anything to warm my feet which are causing me great pain.

There is a gap, no one moves, I glance to either side and find that the coast is clear, now I can make a break for it. I run towards the bed of coals intently focused on my mission and the final goal of the water trough. The two women hold out their hands towards me but I shake them off -not likely, I do this on my own. The impetus is still with me and I march across in four paces, plunging my feet into the trough before I can think about what I'm doing. The incredible heat of the coals fights with the numbing cold of my feet, there is pain but it is not searing, the warm water in the trough is balmy and soothing, strong arms hold mine and I clamber out, a small scalding pinprick on my toe telling me where a piece of charcoal stuck to the skin.

It is over, I rejoin the circle. 'Thanks to the Great goddess for Her support.' my spirit calls upwards into the starlit sky. I am elated and inwardly jumping for joy - I have done it, I have done it, I have walked on fire! I glance back to the firebed, horribly glowing, a raw scarlet gash in the surrounding lawn, and am seized with a feeling of victory, of mastery over pain and fear. I have joined an elite, an ancient brotherhood of Firewalkers, a Mystery has been probed and exposed.

Now candidates are presenting themselves to the fire at an increasing rate, running, walking, skipping across the coals. One young man runs across carrying his baby son - I am horrified - why? what for? There is not time to imagine a possible fall, he is followed by another and then another. One hesitates at the brink and arms reach out to support her, she utters a cry of mixed frustration and anguish and stands aside. One or two who have failed in the past stride bravely across and we are all gladdened on their behalf.

Still the fire burns a livid red, the coals turning white only at the rim; as the embers glow and fade it gives a rippling effect, truly it is alive, a devouring salamander waiting to seize its prey. My elation has transformed itself into a sense of well-being and a hint of pride. Eliza, having established that everyone has had a turn, offers a second chance to walk. I am tempted but no, for me this is a sacred act, not to be cheapened by repetition. Several people make a second attempt, no doubt buoyed up by their earlier triumph. My feet are now too cold to walk much further, the chant has died and it is something of a free-for-all with walkers chasing each other across the coals, approaching from every angle, some dancing euphorically over the embers.

I break away and hobble back indoors where I can thaw out my feet and mull over the ordeal in a quiet corner. Inside there are one or two people who have been unable to walk the coals, one is suffering an asthmatic attack and I give her some healing; in spite of our earlier pep talk there is a significant air of failure and remorse, justifications and excuses fly thick and fast. There is little opportunity for reflection so I make myself useful until the rest of the group return, full of euphoria and chattering excitedly. Now I want to go home and review the evening's achievement in private. I want to ponder on She who gave me strength, on the night sky and the fiery salamander, on the ancient rite that we have just participated in and have perpetuated here in England, thousands of miles away from Pacific Islanders or Indian Braves. As soon as is decently possible I steal away and drive home, my initial feelings now rapidly turning to something more profound.

The following day, after a deep and untroubled sleep, I arise refreshed. As the morning passes I feel the earlier elation returning and by mid-day I am 'swinging from the chandeliers', whooping round the cottage, dancing for joy. The Firewalk symbolised so much more than running across red hot coals, it was a sacred act, an offering to the Great Goddess, a further step up the mystic spiral. I have trans-cended pain, faced the element of fire unsupported and made a deeper commitment to the Path - chosen to follow my instincts rather than the herd and been reward with success. Now I feel like 'one of the big kids' as Eliza was fond of saying.

Groton Wood

I'll never show you Groton Wood
You'll never know its spell
I'll never share the primrose path
That leads beyond the Dell.

The nightingale will sing her song
To me but not to you
As twilight falls alone I'll stand
Beside the silent pool.

The foxglove and the willow herb
May nod their purple heads
This land of faerie magic
Will never know your tread.

The rustling treetops call to me
Long ages we have known
This secret world, this sacred grove
Is mine and mine alone.

I know the narrow pathways
The bluebell's hidden glade
You'll never find your way through here
I'll never show the way.

But maybe when you're older
And wisdom quells your voice
When eyes and ears are all you'll need
A soul that can rejoice.

Then perhaps I'll show you
This enchanted shrine
This private place I love so well
Will then be yours and mine.

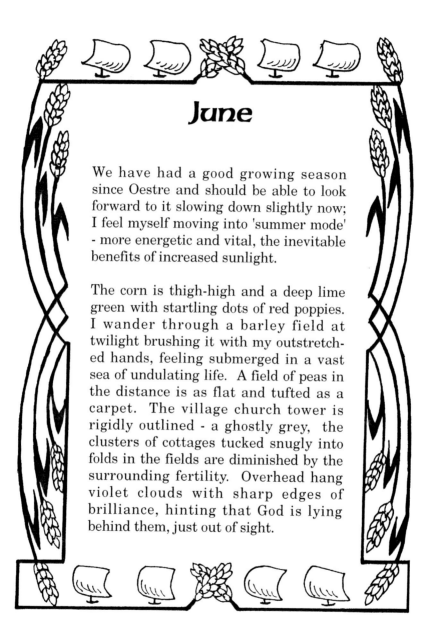

June

We have had a good growing season since Oestre and should be able to look forward to it slowing down slightly now; I feel myself moving into 'summer mode' - more energetic and vital, the inevitable benefits of increased sunlight.

The corn is thigh-high and a deep lime green with startling dots of red poppies. I wander through a barley field at twilight brushing it with my outstretched hands, feeling submerged in a vast sea of undulating life. A field of peas in the distance is as flat and tufted as a carpet. The village church tower is rigidly outlined - a ghostly grey, the clusters of cottages tucked snugly into folds in the fields are diminished by the surrounding fertility. Overhead hang violet clouds with sharp edges of brilliance, hinting that God is lying behind them, just out of sight.

Today I am to visit a nearby park and estate in order to attend a lecture. Prior to us assembling I stroll round the Spinney which shelters the house. Great forest trees have been carefully planted by eighteenth century hands and they now spread out magnificently, one of each native species, each carefully labelled with a small lettered sign nailed to the bole. Oak, elm, chestnut, beech, ash. I survey them all and note the ash tree in particular, memorizing its' features, studying its' shape and design. In the tangle of growth at its' roots I see a small branch, clearly fallen from above. Pulling at it gently and disentangling it from strands of long grass, I reveal what turns out to be a ready made stang. Standing it on end I find it to be about five foot high; there are two well formed prongs sitting evenly on top of a central post, the whole being smoothly proportioned and the wood nicely weathered. What luck! A stang has more or less dropped at my feet, no need to damage a tree in order to cut one, no need to search for an ash, guide book in hand. Here is a tree, labelled clearly 'ash' offering a perfectly made stang for my requirements. Feeling well blessed I transport it to the car - the Goddess has smiled on me once more.

Now my circle can be completed and, after I've peeled off the bark which falls easily into my hands, I await the full moon for consecration.

....

It is time to reconnect with the elements of air and earth and walk the ancient tracks. The Ridgeway is probably one of the oldest drove roads in Europe, crossing the Wiltshire Downs and the crest of the high chalklands leading into Berkshire and finally terminating at Ivinghoe Beacon on the Bucks/Herts border'. For centuries man and beast have traversed this high-way, passing iron-age hill forts, white horses and Neolithic stone formations, viewing the wide skies, gazing down upon open pasture and tiny settlements nestling against the hillside as they have done since time immemorial.

Now I am to join their number and see for myself the 'spinal cord' of southern Britain to which are connected other ancient routes leading in every direction towards the many centres of trade and commerce which are dotted across the land - The Peddars Way, The Icknield Way, The Fosse Way and so on.

I join the Ridgeway at Avebury, its southernmost point. The weather is fairly typical of this time of year - warm sun often overshadowed by billowing clouds. I have packed a rucksack with a very basic selection of clothes and kit which I hope will last me for a few days. Shunning boots which I detest with my heart and soul, I have included two pairs of sandals, one a pair of gold thongs - all I have in my meagre wardrobe. In an ideal world I would travel barefoot but no doubt even Neolithic man had his fur and hide shoes. I have made no plan, have no idea of my return date but just intend to plod along as best I can, savouring the earth below and the sky above, quite unobtainable and free of the pressures of modern society.

A neighbour drives me to Avebury and risks her car up the steep incline that leads to the ridge. She is quite disbelieving of my pilgrimage but I am raring to go; for so many years I have dreamt of this - just me and Mother Nature. At the last minute I find that the weight of the bedroll is too much, I can hardly stand, let alone walk up an incline. It didn't seem to matter when I practiced at home but now I have to make a quick decision and gamble on finding Bed and Breakfast en route. I feel reckless and adventurous, trusting implicitly in the Goddess who will, I hope, provide enough protection to allow me to sample Her joys over the next few days.

Waving jauntily good-bye to my neighbour I take the first steps forward, adjusting my kit and getting used to the unaccustomed burden that will be with me constantly for the next few days. I am quite inexperienced at hiking but, spurred on by the fresh air and wide open spaces, I climb to the top of the ridge and then, turning east, start the long, long journey that will lead to an unknown destination.

There is shale beneath my feet and gathering gloom overhead which speaks of rain to come. I reach the first hill-fort, poised triumphantly above the Wiltshire Downs and briefly explore its environs. My pack is heavy and my sandals reveal every bump in the track but I plod on, refusing to give way to aches and pains. I am accompanied by several walkers, a few mountain bikes and one or two tired old jeeps, there is no chance of being isolated but mercifully no one tries to chat. Soon the track has turned to grass and I am in a less populated area so I find a field gate and brew up tea for a picnic. The experience is not as pleasant as I expected, my first al fresco meal is marred by the prospect of the many miles that stretch ahead - the Ridgeway is eighty miles long. In spite of the lush vegetation and soothing outlook I am eager to get on and cut the break short. In my pack is a selection of wild flower seeds so I dig them out and scatter them wildly, hoping that I have helped to beautify a small corner of England.

Then I am up and off again, anxious to tread the trackway, to explore the great beyond. I am also eager to break through the pain barrier, past the point where physical pains numb and I can fully enjoy the external world. I soon learn the art of plodding, allowing my legs to carry me of their own accord whilst my mind wanders free - across the great green Downs which stretch out below me, sweeping into folds and rising again to the far distance, untouched, open and yet fertile with grass. This must be the same panorama seen by ancient man when he too plodded along here, driving his flocks of sheep to the Midland sheep fairs, sleeping at night in a wood or ditch, kindling fires and washing in streams. My reverie continues for several miles, seeing the body of the Goddess in the green unbroken landscape, soft, rounded and old - primordial and eternal. Always there has been this chalkland, across which thousands of travellers have plodded, diminished by the power and extent of Mother Nature who sleeps here, brushed by clouds, beaten by storms of rain and smiled upon by the life-giving sun. My spirits lift as I travel on.

Later in the day there is driving rain so I drop down from the Ridgeway, taking one of the many intersecting lanes that lead to villages sheltering beneath its protective shoulder. Bed and Breakfast isn't hard to find and I am glad of a bath and a soft bed. Accustomed to walkers, my landlady offers to drive me back up to the Ridgeway the following morning and I gratefully accept, glad to save my strength for the full day's walk ahead.

Once more the weather is mixed but here, high above southern England, away from human contact, I revel in the sudden breezes which send cloud shadows gliding across the hillsides, turning the grassland from pale to dark green, followed by piercing sunbeams blessing the earth with their warmth.

The track ahead is deeply rutted and my feet are developing blisters, the soles punished by each heavy step. To either side lie quiet copses, beckoning me to enter and explore their dark, leafy mysteries. I linger in one or two, absorbed into the stillness, the suspended world of Faerie. There are the remains of a campfire and the encircling trees are carved with primitive faces, leering, grimacing, staring like gargoyles. Here have been held witch rites or similar, others have been drawn to this shady place, a remnant of an abandoned world, high out of reach of modern man.

At noon I reach Wayland Smith, the erstwhile home of the mythical Smith who no doubt shod the pack horses which travelled this route and repaired the iron implements of local farmers. There is a long barrow, turfed over and smoothly rounded, stretching perhaps 100 feet and supported by stone slabs of great antiquity. Enclosing this magical burial ground is a ring of tall beech trees, replacing the original oaks but equally effectively guarding the tomb and no doubt adding to the air of enchantment which is quite tangible to the sensitive. I enter through a kissing gate and, at once, am elevated to a Faerie realm. Here the trees truly whisper, spirits watch from the perimeter of the circle and there is an air of sudden departure as if the place had recently been vacated due to my intruding presence. I pause at the entrance and walk slowly towards the mouth of the barrow. There are bunches of wild flowers placed here, the old worshippers remember their Gods - I too place an offering gleaned from the roadside. Then, softly, mentally on tiptoe, I slowly circle the barrow, aware that I am on hallowed ground, watched perhaps by souls of the undead. At the far end I sit and contemplate the shrine, for that is clearly what it is. Then, casting aside pack and sandals, I dance joyfully from along the entire length, my sore feet soothed by the damp grass, my shoulders freed from their burden, spirits soaring, doing what comes naturally in this enchanted place.

I am gripped by a sense of wonder, just out of reach is another world, my senses stretch to make contact but only brush the fringe, tantalized by longing. I must leave before frustration overcomes me, sadly I retrace my steps to the gate, shouldering my backpack. One last look, hoping to catch a glimpse of an otherworld being but there are only the swaying trees and invisible eyes, the Goddess shields Herself here, only Her breathing is heard.

Onward, onward, the long and winding trail, up hills and down valleys, still I meet other walkers, all of us intent on our own affairs, unwilling to do more than nod at each other, locked into our own private musings. Now, either side of the way are trees and scrubby bushes, only rabbits and a few game birds venture out. It is monotonous and a little smothering. Driven by sheer stubbornness and the lack of any alternative, I trudge mindlessly on, aware that I have completed twenty four hours on the hoof and encouraged to achieve more. Time is by the sun, hunger has left me, pain has settled into a background ache; focused on the road ahead, I sink into a zombie- like state.

A hard pull up a rough hill brings me to a crossroads. Ahead is a breathtaking view of the Berkshire Downs and the gallops of Lambourn, a tamer and more shallow land than I have seen so far. Civilization in the shape of tarmac crosses my path but although a comforting presence, I am not tempted to rejoin it. For miles ahead the Ridgeway extends into the distance, a clear and winding hilltop path, bathed in sunlight, inviting me to venture along its length.

Tramping on, I reach springy turf. A mild breeze seduces me and I remove two layers of clothing. Skylarks soar upwards, flowers bloom on the verge and a bare-chested man strides by, plainly exhilarating in the freedom of the great outdoors. I watch him disappear over the near horizon, envious of his masculine privilege. A few paces more and I discard both inhibitions and tee-shirt, then off with the bra and I am following in his footsteps, bare-breasted and as liberated as he. The warmth of the sun on my flesh, the breeze caressing my nipples and wafting across my naked back is a tremendous experience. I carry my kitbag on one shoulder, filled with renewed vitality and revelling in a closer walk with nature. The grassy track continues and I swing along, now quite accustomed to the isolation and feeling truly re-connected with the powers of earth and air.

This blissful interlude doesn't last long, however. Soon a group of walkers appear in the distance and I am obliged to respect custom by re-clothing myself. After a while dark clouds obscure the sun and I once again finish my journey drenched in rain, seeking shelter in a sympathetic Bed and Breakfast.

Again I am driven back up to the ridge the following morning. As I am now approaching the more heavily populated areas the track becomes busier. Now there are dog walkers and horse riders; seldom am I out of sight of someone, which is of some comfort I suppose. The terrain gets easier but the views are less spectacular. Skies clear and I am bathed in sunlight, Hill Forts and White Horses are left behind and the roadway slopes gently down to the Thames Valley. Sheep are grazing behind long stretches of wire fencing, late lambs are gamboling and running shyly away when I try to make friends.

I have realized that eighty miles is much too far for my frail body to walk and have decided to curtail my trip as and when appropriate. My step has become quite rhythmic but it is lacking any sort of bounce and I see little point in mindlessly tramping for the sake of it. With this decision behind me I feel more cheerful and once again enjoy the journey. At this point the ridge is quite distinct and sharply etched, on one side there is a steep drop down to a plain, stretching endlessly into the distance, and on the other are meadows and fenced pasturage. There is greater detail in the scenery - distant roads dotted with moving traffic, cooling towers, sprawling villages and public buildings. The wild, untamed world of the Goddess has here felt the hand of Man, scale has been reduced to human size, Her body has been landscaped into a more manageable form.

Ahead lies the outskirts of a town, I expect my route to bypass it and content myself with drinking in the view. One or two grooms are walking their horses over the turf nearby, looking solemn and businesslike, apparently quite unaware of their marvellous surroundings; if I had their job I would enjoy it a great deal more than they appear to do. On reaching a small stream I settle myself behind a hedge and brew up, relaxed now that a large proportion of my journey is behind me. Fully shod I paddle in the water, not a soul in sight, just a collection of antiquated storage barns.

After a brief rest I continue on my journey, the Ridgeway has become a rough road now, wide and partially stone surfaced. Travelling towards me are two expensive looking four-track vehicles, three young men sitting three abreast in each. As they approach I catch sight of their faces and am shocked at such evil expressions, perhaps they are on drugs of some sort. They leer as they pass, turning round in their seats, fixing me with purposeful looks, talking amongst themselves, unsmiling, rough and wild looking. I look away, hoping they will lose interest, but the vehicles slow to a crawl. This is a desolate spot and there is no cover, not a tree nor a ditch; for once there are no walkers in sight. The cars slowly disappear over the horizon and I relax for a moment, still plodding on under the now relentless glare of the sun. Then, back they come - they have turned round and are cruising threateningly over the brow of a slight hill. It is clear that they mean business, all eyes are glued on me, sensations of panic surge through my bones and my head starts pounding. Slowly they approach, bouncing over the rough ground like great jungle beasts closing in on their prey.

In this awful moment my surroundings take on an air of menace - the sunshine is harsh, birdsong mocking and the pleasant green expanse of the gallops merely an empty space, a useless void offering no protection from my predators. There is movement around me but inside I have reached that place of dead stillness which all cornered animals find. The cars slow to a halt before me and I gaze in disbelief at the depraved look in their eyes and their intense expressions. They mean business - not rape or pillage but both and probably something more deadly besides. I am helpless and powerless, a perfect victim. Then, without warning, there is a sudden revving up of engines and they roar away in a cloud of dust, avoiding my eyes, staring straight ahead, anxious to depart. In their wake, innocently striding along, is the squaddy I spoke to yesterday, tall and well built, all highly tanned brawn and little brain; he is going home to visit his mother who lives in north Berkshire. Still petrified and quite immobile I watch him pass by; we nod in recognition, he quite unaware of the drama he has interrupted. My instincts are to fall upon him in gratitude, kissing that chiselled chin, hugging that striped T-shirt, sobbing on his broad shoulders. Instead I send fervent thanks to the Goddess and then bolt for cover as fast as my legs will carry me. Along the track, down into a hollow and then a quick dash across open land which leads me mercifully to a roadway and a glimpse of human habitation, cottages nestling in the trees and sleepy summer gardens. I have somehow forgotten my aching limbs and heavy backpack and in the shelter of a village lane I crash out on the verge, struggling to regain my breath, wanting to sink into the lush green earth.

Slowly I regain my equilibrium and my senses become less acute. I am badly shaken though and too weak to carry on at present. Still feeling vulnerable I decide to find the nearest pub and reconsider my plans; at the bottom of the hill is just what I'm looking for and I order a medicinal brandy. The landlord tells me that I must travel through Goring on Thames if I am to continue my journey; the prospect of mindlessly trudging along urban pavements, assaulted by traffic fumes and jostling crowds fills me with horror. Suddenly I am overcome by wave after wave of homesickness - for my little cottage, my cat and my garden - I have had enough.

Wearily shouldering my kitbag I drag my aching feet towards a nearby bus-stop. There is a long wait and I pass the time numbly gazing into space, too overwrought to think clearly. Eventually a dear little bus trundles into view and I climb thankfully aboard. We travel jauntily along under the ridge, in and out of pink thatched villages, past cornfields and meadows until we come to Avebury. In two hours we have covered a journey that has taken me three days.

I reflect on my adventure, the earth which has spread itself out before me so grandly in panoramic views and more humbly in the shape of a dirt track that has carried me across the ancient Downland; the air which has filled my lungs, ruffled my hair and blown great white clouds across my horizons. I consider the Dark God in the shape of predatory men in Land Rovers and the Great Goddess who saved me from a fate worse than death. I have danced in Faerie realms and walked bare-breasted over sunny hilltops, I have shouldered my burden and walked my own pathway unsupported by humans, seen raw power in the wind and rain and followed in the footsteps of my ancestors. I have indeed forged links with Her, the Great Mother, She who rules the tides and the elements, protector of women. My journey has not been in vain.

....

Tonight, under the light of the full moon I place my smooth, dry stang out in the garden, upright in the soil. Taking a bowl of salted water I cleanse it by sprinkling and then, with a smudge stick, outline its limbs with smoking sage, asking for a blessing on this 'altar' and dedicating it to the work of the Great Goddess. That done, I 'shoe' it by hammering a nail into the tip of the upright, earthing its power. Then it is laid away for my next visit to the woods.

....

For many years I have been fascinated by the ceremony of drawing down the moon. I recently met a male witch who appeared to take a shine to me and was happy to discuss occult matters - a rare occurrence amongst those on the Hidden Path. Rupert is his name and he claims to be a hereditary witch although I have some misgivings about that, he is rather too flamboyant to hail from such a persecuted quarter of society. However, not long after I had made his acquaintance I asked him if he had ever drawn down the moon and, in his usual expansive manner, he replied 'Of course, lots of times'. I was a little taken aback at his speedy reply but took the opportunity to ask if he would do it for me and he unhesitatingly replied that he would be happy to do so at any time. After making so many fruitless enquiries in the past I was dismayed at such a show of co-operation but thanked him nevertheless and suggested the full moon in July which will fall in my birth sign of Capricorn. He readily agreed and we exchanged telephone numbers for future reference.

To my great surprise he phoned me last night to remind me of our plan. It has been arranged that the rite be performed at his house, rather than out of doors which I would have preferred, but I am still eager to try it and be guided by one more experienced than I.

....

It is midsummer and the world outside vibrates in an ecstatic triumph of creation. Overhead the sun radiates a fiery heat, its rays penetrating every shadowy corner. The birds respond in joyful song from branch and nest, swooping across the sky to proclaim their praises from another perch. Frenzied insects swarm in clouds or chirp heedlessly amidst their leafy foraging. In the dancing breeze the corn is swept to and fro and trees undulate, revealing fresh shades of green as their leaves relentlessly flutter.

My spirits soar on the current and dance in unison with the Goddess as She displays her summer splendour. Today Her peak of fertility has been reached and as Her priestess I am caught up in the celebration. Nearby Silbury Hill, a Neolithic mound, represents the body of the Great Mother and it is to this shrine that I am drawn today in order to re-affirm my part in the creative process.

The car journey is frustrating, to be enclosed on such a day as this is tortuous. However, as I climb through the Wiltshire Downs with pale green sweeps all around me and silky blue skies above, I cannot help uttering a whoop of sheer pleasure. As always the sense of ancient man and ancient ways cloaks the hills, so mottled with sunshine and shadow, so deserted and timeless. One feels as if one could walk these ridges and summits unto the very gates of heaven. Silbury Hill lies ahead, a smoothly rounded artificial mound, made by man in praise of woman - of fertility and motherhood and all that adorns the earth with flower and fruit. Like so many tourist attractions it is fenced off and prohibited to the public, but I am not the first worshipper to scale the fence and risk contravening a bye-law in order to return to the Mother's womb.

It is a rough, steep climb up a narrow path which winds through coarse meadow grass. Below me I spy coach loads of European tourists who are clearly visiting ancient sites today, dutifully admiring West Country earthworks of which they have no real comprehension. I keep a low profile to avoid detection and, as exhilaration mixes with breathlessness, I finally arrive, gasping, at the summit.

For some time I lie on my back in the long grass, quite out of sight, alone in the lap of the Goddess. Around me the sounds of summer, which had initially prompted this pilgrimage, buzz and sing, whisper and sigh. Here I feel suspended between the earth mother and the sky father, cradled in a billowing elemental nest. It is 'back to the womb' indeed, a fitting place to be at the Solstice.

With no one else around I am able to slip off my clothes and bask in the mid-day sun, soaking up the rays that have been so weak and oblique up until now. I bury my face in the long grass, sniffing deeply the scent of hay and baked earth. Overhead two jet planes scream past, tearing through the ancient membrane - but peace is restored and soon the swallows are back, darting thither and yon, seeking insects for their mid-day meal.

Thoroughly toasted and re-vitalised with vitamin C, I take a languid look at the landscape, leaning back on my elbows, my hair a hot and wispy tangle. To the west lies the Avebury Circle, a familiar sight after my recent Ridgeway trek. I follow the processional way to West Kennett with my eyes and note a crop circle in the middle distance. This is surely a contemporary sign of summer, an indication of greater powers at work, mystifying us all with their illicit and stealthy visitations. The symbol offered to the downs of Wiltshire this year is precise in its geometry and compellingly abstract. I ponder for some moments on its symbolism but fail in my comprehension and turn over, chin on hands, to contemplate the vast green plains that grace the northern aspect. Here the Goddess is untouched in Her splendour. Long before mankind discovered this chalkland and tramped its' grassy crests, so the fertile land produced lush, verdant meadows, rich pasture and endless rolling hills, folding gently one into another, softened by time into a pleasing display of the earth as she was originally created, the Great Mother's body lying rounded and abundant under the eternal blue of the sky.

Here, on this day, in this place, naked and sun-soaked I too desire to offer up abundance. There is no lover, nor consort here, to share with me the creative flow that pulses through the earth at this time. I am unable to unite with the God and

Goddess in celebrating another season of successful reproduction but I am still urged to add my voice to the blend of song and symphony that soars with the skylark and whispers on the wind.

Impulsively I rise to my feet and stand in a pose of adoration, arms outstretched, legs apart, my head thrown back to face the sky - adlibbing in true oracular fashion I cry:

'O Great Goddess, Summer Queen
Around me lies a veil of green
Beneath my feet an earthly womb
The world is decked with nature's blooms.
Regard your child, your priestess true
My heart and soul submit to you
Caress me with your fertile kiss
Bestow on me midsummer bliss.'

There is a pause as my words float away on the breeze. I stand rigid and exalted, the sun warming each hidden fold of my body, penetrating the dark recesses so rarely exposed, opening up pores and pockets of mystery, exciting feminine fluids into unrestricted flux Then there is a tremor and a spark and slowly a light pulse travels from head to foot, brushing my soul and tingling my senses. It vanishes into the earth leaving me shaken but invigorated, strung like a freshly tuned bow string. I sink to the ground in limp gratitude 'Thank you Goddess' The words are muttered, the teardrops fall to earth, the spell is broken. I reach for my clothes, distracted and suddenly meek but at the same time shot through with renewed vitality, blessed and caressed. Sleepily, dreamily I start my descent, reluctant to leave this sacred place but anxious to reflect on my moment of transcendence in a private space. Inwardly I am filled with delight, outwardly I am just another trespasser climbing over the fence and back into harsh reality.

Midsummer follows closely upon the heels of the summer solstice; the two occasions mark the beginning and the end of that few days when fertility is at its peak, the opposite of the winter solstice/Yule celebration when all is quite dead and inert. During this period the days appear to get longer and longer, darkness being reserved for only a few hours during the dead of night. In fact daylight hours remain the same length for this brief interval before imperceptibly shortening as we begin plunging down towards the autumn equinox. The increased daylight has the effect of making one particularly active and, after such a successful solstice I am eager to add to the celebrations by marking midsummer day by a trip to a sacred site.

Knowlesworth Henge is about two hours' drive away, but amidst this delightful weather the journey is no hardship and I drink in the changing views as I whizz through three counties to find myself deep in the Hampshire border. I find the site quite easily, and after parking the car, admire the circular ditch and note the deserted church standing in the centre. Here our Christian forefathers have tried and failed. Somewhat crassly they have attempted to overpower and dominate a very ancient place of worship by crudely superimposing their own on top. The result has been an abject failure - the church has long been ruined but the henge is still perfectly formed and well maintained by the nation, paganism has triumphed yet again.

I approach with care and slowly start to circle the henge. My attention is caught by a courting couple lying side by side in the middle of the mound, sunbathing and no doubt taking a break from their journey. I continue to pace the ditch, now barefoot and somewhat entranced, speculating on the origins of this place and the scenes it must have witnessed over the years. After a few minutes the ditch becomes more shallow and the courting couple move more clearly into view. I cannot fail to notice them and realize that their sunbathing in such a sacred place has aroused the God and Goddess in them both and they are now amorously locked into an embrace. A dozen or so steps further and my meditations are broken again by movement; I look up - the woman is clearly not satisfied with a few innocent kisses and is shamelessly seducing her mate who lies unconcernedly on his back. As I watch I see that she is clearly overcome with lust and it is not long before she has them both unbuttoned and rhythmically moving at an increasing pace. Startled I look round and check for other visitors, something they clearly haven't considered. There is nobody here but me and, although it occurs to me to make my presence felt in some way, I realize that they are unlikely to hear me, so engrossed are they in each other, shamelessly, blatantly coupling under the midsummer sunshine, performing an ancient pagan ritual in an ancient pagan temple.

Somewhat taken aback I continue my circumnambulations, hidden by the high earthworks. When I again reach the entrance I stop to see if I can now be accepted into this place, wishing to explore the mound and the ruins, hoping to survey the landscape and ponder on our Neolithic ancestors. But no, still the sacred marriage continues, two now as one, she astride her partner, lost to reality, unaware of everything but the rising tide of desire that has gripped them both. They have truly claimed this place as their own, doing what comes naturally, obeying the pulse of life as it trembles and thunders through the earth at this high point of fecundity. Who am I to oppose the Great Goddess in all Her glory, no doubt this ancient site has seen many such acts of love as this. I creep away and head for home.

....

A free day and a glorious one, sunshine and balmy breezes. I make my way to the woods after lunch. The bluebells have long since vanished but in other ways there has been a lot of growth since my last visit. Around me is a strong feeling of vitality, of sap gushing through trees and plants alike, of buds emerging and blooms exploding. Over it all is still the benign presence of the Lady - the Faerie Queen - coaxing, protecting, ruling with a firm and gentle hand.

I follow the familiar path and reach the stream, now a little slower in its movement. I cross over and walk deeper into the woods, pigeons bursting into flustered flight, treetops sighing and creaking with the weight of new growth. The oak tree is straight ahead and, beneath its shady boughs, is my circle, untouched and waiting for me. I brush it clear with the little tuft of broom that I keep tucked into a crevice in the trunk and erect my stang at the northernmost point. Now it is complete and I can use it all summer for my meditations.

The breeze drops and birdsong fills the air, I cast the circle under the warm afternoon sun and sink into meditation. Somewhere on the edge of my vision the Faerie Queen is nodding approval - a sacred space in a sacred place.

The Breath of Life

O give me the wild wild wind
Show me a blustering gale
Take me to hills where the air blows free
And tell me of billowing sails.

Let me bask in the zephyrs of summer
Let me stride through the swaying corn
Let me lift up my face to the chasing clouds
'Twas surely for this I was born.

A storm on the distant horizon
The calm as the menace grows near

Then eddies and squalls and the thunder
I am there when the Gods re-appear.

O set my two feet on the fore-deck
Let me lean near to the prow
May the tingling of masts reassure me
That the wind is still keeping her vow.

When hurricanes rage may I waken
Where heather is blown may I tread
If God is our guide and creator
Should His breathing e're cease we are dead.

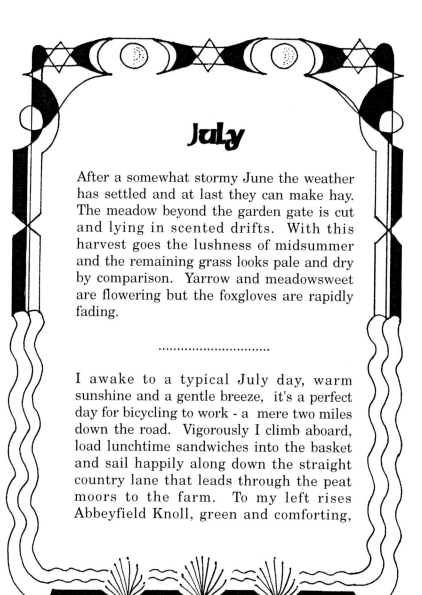

July

After a somewhat stormy June the weather has settled and at last they can make hay. The meadow beyond the garden gate is cut and lying in scented drifts. With this harvest goes the lushness of midsummer and the remaining grass looks pale and dry by comparison. Yarrow and meadowsweet are flowering but the foxgloves are rapidly fading.

....

I awake to a typical July day, warm sunshine and a gentle breeze, it's a perfect day for bicycling to work - a mere two miles down the road. Vigorously I climb aboard, load lunchtime sandwiches into the basket and sail happily along down the straight country lane that leads through the peat moors to the farm. To my left rises Abbeyfield Knoll, green and comforting, dappled with sunlight; in the foreground cows gently graze the rich pasture and the moor gives way to thick copses, dark green and boggy. Untamed trees clasp their upper branches together, woodbine and ivy romp resolutely through scrub and brushwood. Here there is a hint of the primeval - wild woodland deeply choked with aboriginal vegetation, shading deer and badger and perhaps something nearly human.

I glide smoothly past, watching closely for signs of life, as always feeling like a trespasser on foreign land, instinctively knowing that this is not my natural habitat in spite of my curiosity. Two ducks run across the road and overhead the sun streams through clouds, illuminating the road ahead, an ancient causeway across the moors, built to carry foot travellers from one Neolithic settlement to another through winter swamp and summer meadow.

The journey is not long and soon I turn into the farm gate, freewheeling into the yard, somewhat overheated but full of summer splendour. I park the bike and walk across to the office carrying my sandwiches. Once inside I realize that I am in for a bad day; Carol my colleague is carping already and it's only 9:00 a.m. She turns on me and we have the first minor confrontation which I manage to scale down to a disagreement and finally dismiss with a cheerful remark. She goes off, mildly steaming and I take a few moments to gaze across the moor, framed in our large picture windows. As I watch the light and shade playing upon the dark brown peat so thick black clouds gather in the west and in no time at all the sunny day is overcast and heavy drops of rain splash wildly down from the sky, splattering on the windows and creating shallow puddles in the yard - the storms are with us still.

By 10:00 a.m. there is a deluge and I gaze gloomily out onto a landscape already waterlogged and severely obscured by sheets of rain. Carol is still in carping mode and, upon discovering that I have biked to work, unleashes a volley of mocking comments.

At lunchtime the storm has intensified, sweeping wildly across the countryside, dark clouds pregnant with rain, mud oozing across the road and rivulets cascading off buildings. Drains are blocked, cars splash through surface water and all the time the gloom gathers as overcast skies deepen and the tempest rages.

Carol makes the most of it, maliciously noting that I have no coat and my bicycle is thoroughly rain sodden. Securely in possession of a company car, she spends most of the afternoon childishly crowing at my anticipated misfortune. I ignore her as best I can but am only too bleakly aware that I face an impossible journey home. Nevertheless I feel sure that somehow my predicament will be taken care of - 'there is a blessing on those who serve' and as I have put myself in the hands of the Gods I must rely on Them to assist me in one way or another.

On and on thunders the storm throughout the afternoon, relentlessly flooding all within its wake. Equally relentless is Carol; with no opposition from me she builds up to a crescendo of derision, now gazing triumphantly out of the window then tripping across the office to gain a better view of my expected Waterloo. I hang on grimly, my faith in deliverance unshaken, silently continuing with my work. At 4:45, my faith still holding strong, I glance up at the sky and perceive a faint western light; inwardly smiling I finish my work and clear my desk. Five minutes later the rain ceases and a blinding sun emerges from behind storm clouds - Carol, who has been intently watching the sky all day, falls silent; I gather my lunchbox and handbag together. At 5:00 p.m. the world is bathed in veils of glory. 'Good night Carol' I say pointedly, looking her straight in the eye, taking in her stunned, open-mouthed astonishment. I saunter out to my bicycle. With a quick wipe of the saddle I am soon aboard and happily peddling home, lifting my face to catch the golden rays, revelling in the prismatic charm of the rain-washed moorland and thanking the Gods for protecting and sustaining me yet again.

....

Giant umbelliferous surge up along the roadside like triffids. Mauve scabious and pink and white yarrow crowd bloated campion, its white petals dropping. The nettles are heavy with green flowers, the cow parsley is now skeletal, brown and dry. Already seed heads are forming in the hedgerows, entwined by pink columbine fluted like a gored skirt. In the fields rogue stems of wild oats shake their heads above the corn as it dips and sways. I roam the lanes after dark watching the stars appear, soaking up the warmth of the earth and breathing in the sense of fulfilment that lies all around. As I sit on the roadside smothered in long grass and summer flowers the full moon rises slowly overhead, its rays reaching down to me like a silvery pathway that I cannot travel. My spirit rises in an attempt at transcendence but 'I cannot, cannot go'.

....

Tonight Rupert and I are going to attempt to draw down the moon so I pack a white robe and other accessories and, after work, drive to Emmersleigh where he lives. This is my first trip to Devon for a long time so I avoid the motorway and follow a more minor road which leads its winding way through small country towns and pretty villages. The levels of Somerset and the hills of Devon are full of light and shadow as the sun starts to sink on the western horizon and I meander rather slowly up hill and down dale to Emmersleigh. In my recent meditations I have visualised Rupert's cottage as one of a row of colour washed dwellings built on a sloping side street with countryside beyond. Now, as I enter the Emmersleigh, I make enquiries for Jonah Street, only to be directed to a seedy row of villas in the centre of town. Lenten Cottage turns out to be the grimmest one of all with grubby net curtains at the window and shabby paintwork. There is no sign of life and I am shocked at this scenario which has all the attributes of a low budget horror film. Fortunately I have informed a mutual friend of my whereabouts and, if I am whisked away to join the white slave trade, there is someone who would go to the Authorities.

After the second knock, in true 'B' movie style, the door slowly opens and I catch a glimpse of a black robed figure behind the outstretched hand grasping the edge of the door. Rupert's dark face and, I suspect, newly dyed black hair appears - we are clearly in for a dramatic evening. I feel my chakras closing down in self-defence and step over the threshold. The house is expectedly musty and none too clean. 'Come into my temple' says Rupert in a deep bass voice - he is in sinister mode tonight. I gingerly follow him down the gloomy hallway, matchboarding on the walls and faded brown lino on the floor. He opens the door with a flourish and I step in. 'Take your shoes off!' he hisses abruptly and I dutifully slip them off.

The 'Temple' turns out to be the back parlour, furnished with a dingy 1960s three piece suite, a carpet of indeterminate colour but gritty texture and a coal-effect fire hastily shoved into the fireplace. Above us is an enormous round Chinese lampshade which swings low and dominates the room, making it difficult to cross from one side to the other. In the corner is a cat litter tray. A single window overlooks a tiny backyard enclosed by Victorian red brick walls; there is a hint of darkening sky above, the only access to the natural world in this grim place. I glance across to the open kitchen door - white appliances are loaded with dirty dishes, the table top cooker is streaked with baked-on cooking spills and a damp wooden floor is revealed through moth eaten tiles.

What am I doing in this threadbare little den of iniquity, so reminiscent of a newspaper exposé of a Satanic cult? I feel that I have bitten off too much here.

As I sit down carefully, a warm heavy creature jumps onto my lap, I look down and smother a gasp - it is a hairless cat! Rupert laughs and introduces 'Pelham', his 'familiar'. Pelham purrs and settles himself down, revealing his wrinkled skin which I view with distaste. I find him most 'unfamiliar'. Biting the bullet I offer a stroke and he responds ecstatically, burying himself further, hotly craving my affection. Trapped, I survey the room again and agree to a cup of coffee. Rupert potters about in the kitchenette. 'I've been wearing this all day' he says breezily, referring to his heavy black velvet robe. 'So useful in the heat'. Having gained my full attention he proceeds to name-drop furiously, pointing out statuettes and artifacts given to him by prominent people in the occult world. There appears to be no-one he doesn't know and nowhere he hasn't been - all this for my benefit, a self confessed novice. He continues to parade his insecurities as we drink our coffee, I listen carefully but view him objectively, seeing the little boy behind the showman and wondering how I can get this rite performed in a satisfactory manner after having gone to such trouble to get here.

I finish my coffee and idly rest the empty cup on the shabby sofa cushion. 'Don't do that!' cries Rupert, rushing across with a coaster. 'It'll mark the sofa.' I am speechless at his implied criticism and pointedly place my empty cup on the table. The cat slopes across the room and makes full and odourous use of the litter tray. In utter disgust I reach for my car keys, but a moment later, out of a perverse mixture of morbid curiosity and distaste I decide to brave it out. After all, this has been a long-awaited occasion.

Time passes, darkness falls and Rupert produces a bottle of wine. Moonrise is at 9:00 p.m. and I get fidgety as he downs glass after glass. I fail to see how one can expect to achieve an altered state of consciousness whilst earthbound with alcohol and refuse to join him. It seems likely from his smouldering looks that seduction is his aim and I resolve to take magical matters into my own hands. Unable to agree on a suitable time to begin, I leave him consulting the ephemeris and go into the next room to change into my robe. This room is equally musty and dingy, filled with framed certificates of achievement and self portraits from which I am able to establish 'Rupert's' real name, which I file away for future reference.

Returning to the 'Temple' I rather crossly remind him that we should proceed at 9:00.p.m. realising by now that his reluctance is due to ineptitude, clearly this one's going to be on me. Eventually he finishes his glass and attempts to dress the altar, explaining in unnecessary detail just where each piece was obtained and which well-known occultist bequeath- ed it to him. It is a long drawn out affair. Keeping calm in order to remain receptive to any magical forces we may attract, I nevertheless smirk inwardly as I am obliged to obey his barrack room commands. 'Take this candle and follow me round the circle' he barks, bumping into the monstrous lampshade and falling over. He is drunk and shoots me a shameful, embarrassed look. When he is upright once more we re-commence at a more gentle pace, following the usual routine of establishing the quarters. In a low voice Rupert invokes the Lady and we stand facing one another. There is a pause in the proceedings and I take this opportunity to silently issue my own invocation, drawing a circle of light around myself and focusing my mind on the astral realms. I have totally written off Rupert's abilities and now attempt to make direct contact in a more respectful manner.

At this point Rupert kneels to give me the five-fold kiss which he clearly feels is a momentous event and expects a reaction of indefinable magnitude. I hold myself in a state of equilibrium, neither in one world or another, my mind objectively balanced - ready but not expectant.

'Blessed be thy feet that have brought thee in these ways
Blessed be thy knees that shall bend at Her sacred altar
Blessed by thy womb without which we should not be
Blessed be thy breast formed in beauty in strength
Blessed be thy lips that shall utter the sacred names.'

Rupert is well past his prime and, with creaking knees and much heavy breathing, he completes the ancient prayer and raises himself back to a standing position. I am quite unmoved by this and there is a further silent pause. Then, looking rather foolish, he gently takes my hands and lifts my arms into a horizontal position. Unexpectedly I feel a sense of buoyancy arising from beneath my feet, travelling up through my body and spreading across into my outstretched arms. They lift and drop, apparently of their own accord, and then drop again, lift again and drop, continuing to rise and now fall in a wave-like movement.

Rupert drops to his knees on the floor, staring up at me in amazement. He may be acting again or he may be truly overawed at this phenomena, I am now quite indifferent, poised in some unreal transcendent space, a mild electric-like power drawing up from beneath my feet, elevating my arms and discharging through my fingertips. He no doubt sees more than I am aware of.

I slip out of time, eyes half-closed, feeling the current travelling up my body in steady waves. There is no increase of power, it is rhythmic and unvarying, propelling my outstretched arms in slow flapping wing-like motions. Neither is there any exertion on my part, no heaviness from standing in this 'crucifix' position; outwardly I remain quite balanced although I am inwardly a little elated by this beating pulse. As always in magic, my critical, questioning faculties have been suspended and my will surrendered. However, I am a trifle surprised that power is drawn from below, rather than from above as one would expect from the moon.

My arms continue to undulate of their own accord, my fingertips tingling with undischarged power. I am aware of Rupert's presence, but from a far distance, he is beyond some great chasm that has opened out between us. Nevertheless I reach across and rest my hands briefly on his head in a gesture of blessing or healing; he mutters some words of gratitude, looking raptly upwards, and I resume my palpitations.

There is no passage of time, all is the eternal now. Ripples run from feet to fingertips, my arms involuntarily rising as the power rises, dropping as it is discharged, on and on. I feel as if I have linked into some kind of universal perpetual motion, a conductor or conduit for celestial energies.

Then Rupert stirs and the silence is broken. I dimly recall my will which is at rest in some far corner of my being. With a little effort I reduce my arm movements until they are hanging by my side and open my eyes fully. Still there is a small pulse running through me but as I attempt to walk forward I break the circuit and it ceases. Rupert and I look at each other wordlessly and I stumble outside to sit in the backyard, now cool and dark, still somewhat entranced and incommunicable, eager to view the moon with which I am still connected.

Rupert has dropped his condescending air. He brings me a cup of coffee and glides away, leaving me in peace. As always it takes me a long time to fully return to my body and I am still vague when he finally joins me some time later.

'You looked about sixteen standing there' he says, 'you were being overshadowed by the maiden.'

'I certainly felt very buoyant' I reply, reflecting that it is indeed only in maidenhood that one feels quite as I had done. Perhaps he is right for once.

When I am more myself Rupert wants an account of the experience and I do my best to oblige, although there is little to elucidate and no words to express the magic of the rite. He is surprisingly considerate as I try to explain the inexplicable, groping for words and gazing into the middle distance, unwilling to surrender completely to reality.

It is very late, hours have passed in minutes and midnight is near. I make plans to leave before Rupert decides to take advantage of my semi-conscious state with further ideas of seduction. Back in everyday clothes I feel more like myself and, after a brief good-bye, I venture out into the dark, sad little street. As I drive away I glance to my left and see a side-street edged with traditional Devon cottages sloping away to the moor. It is the street I have been seeing in my meditations, not quite Rupert's neighbourhood, but close.

At this time of night the roads are deserted and I am home in an hour, clear-headed and immensely satisfied with the evening's work. I have drawn down the Maiden and retained my 'maidenhood'. Overhead the Lady moon gleams brightly down in the sign of Capricorn, sending out gentle waves of power, woman to woman. Once again I feel truly blessed.

Elemental

Running through the darkness
Shunning thoughts of Man
Answering the summons of
A blue-green misty hand.

Breathlessly on tiptoe
Overwhelmed and awed
I pause in silent homage
At Nature's secret hoard.

Above lies black diamante
Ahead the whispering marsh
The slipping secret river
A bird cry lone and harsh.

Moonlight tinges reed beds
A tall and trembling throng
Protecting tender creatures
Who pierce the night with song.

Such vastness shrinks my stature
Eternity unfurled.
And Man is surely trespassing
In this nocturnal world.

O lead me to my coracle
That I may gently row
Meandering and dreaming
Where fenland rivers flow.

And stars will smile their blessing
And warblers call to me
Caressing reeds will comfort
As I sail to the sea.

August

Wheat stands high, golden heads bent, as restless as a football crowd; purple thistles unite in a bristling barrier, trees rise like galleons in a sea of rustling corn. Meadowsweet froths yellow on the verges, patches of mayweed droop untidily, more suited to a garden patch than the roadside. Hollyhocks nod against cottage walls, rusty decaying leaves, the flowers chasing each other up the stems. In the air there is an imperceptible stillness, we are at a turning point - summer is ending and autumn will soon begin.

Long shadows betray the slow decline towards the years' end. The harvest is in full swing, the countryside a patchwork of muted colours. Everywhere is an air of surrender and a tranquillity born of completion.

Lughnasadh now, the 'season of mellow fruitfulness', the moment of fulfilment when crops and fruit are harvested, when a large golden moon hangs in the sky and every growing thing has reached a point of perfection: each garden flower, each ear of corn, each round red rowan berry.

....

This morning Jester, the cat, chases a sparrow into the kitchen and, as a result of frantic efforts to escape and my hysterical shouting it manages to lodge itself behind the boiler. Horrified, I evict the cat and switch everything off. With torch in hand I search vainly for the little creature but it is well and truly trapped, flattened between wall and aluminium. There is a long wait whilst I try to figure out a way to release him from this death by pressing. Eventually I take another look and find that he is still alive and has eased his way along the cleft by his claws. I am impressed by such intelligence and hope that he has the stamina to continue. Still I am unable to assist and I must allow him further time to calm down and make his own way - he is out of my reach. Finally, unable to stand the suspense any longer I take another look and find him still wedged but further along the chasm, heroically easing himself nearer and nearer to freedom. A few minutes more and I reach for a ruler, gingerly nudging the little body until he is free of the boiler. Without a backward glance he soars through the open door, winging his way over the garden and up into the blue, unscathed and released from prison. Jester wanders nonchalantly back inside and I can't resist a few sharp words in her direction.

....

This is not a season to be celebrated on one night only. It must be savoured and drunk deeply of, drowsy day and dusky night embraced and absorbed. Each day another field is shorn and the crop baled. Fruits are turning black and scarlet; in the orchards there is an increased hum of activity. I survey the changing scene and sniff the air, savouring the ripeness of the earth and the bounty of our most gracious Lady. This is also 'Mabon', an old Celtic term:

> 'With corn this altar's blessed
> The earth is laid to rest
> A final sigh
> Now soon to die
> The Goddess seeks Her rest.'

....

A balmy night with glittering stars studding a deep blue sky, I stand and gaze at the firmament and the glories of heaven. Shooting stars drop through the darkness, one after another. Sirius is well risen and shining keenly - we are in the midst of the Dog Days. Far away a vixen cries and instantly the local dogs bark in response.

....

It is hot, hot, hot - sticky and sultry. All day I have sat behind the picture window in our office slowly cooking in the heat. The peat moor is gently smoking, the result of months of accumulated warmth and everywhere there is limp foliage, drowsy flies and dusty tracks. Everyone is only too glad to leave promptly and by 5:15 the site is deserted. I saunter slowly towards the rhyne where my boat is moored and sit on the plank bridge trying to catch the slight breeze which plays across the water. Nature is at a standstill, hovering in the scorching summer sun, wilting under the fiery gaze. Even the insects have sought the shade and all is motionless.

For some time I sit in contemplation watching the water as it ripples and glistens. The rhyne is only about 15' wide, straight sided and no more than 4' deep. The water is peat brown but clear and free from detritus since the NRA dragged it clean last month. On the banks is a coagulated strip of waste, a mixture of congealed plant life and the odd beer can, heavily sprinkled with pearly mussel shells swept in from the sea some twenty miles distant. A dead fish or two adds to the mixture.

It is quite silent across the moor, not a trace of human life, most people are no doubt enjoying a cold drink on the patio. I wander over to the bank and find a clean strip to sit on. Then, with a quick glance round, I impulsively pull off my clothes and slither down into the water; it closes round me as I gasp with mild shock. The water is warm but the contrast between my earlier stickiness and this cool, mellifluous state, is marked. I am exhilarated. Plunging deeply, I find that my toes touch the bottom - a sensuous layer of mud; I can stand with the water covering my shoulders, unseen and yet seeing, a river sprite, naked and flowing with the current. Pure pleasure wells up within me and I duck and swirl, fresh fronds caressing my limbs, silky wavelets easing away the dust and tension of the day. I have no desire to engage in any serious swimming, this is a delicious bathe, a refreshing, regenerative plunge amidst Nature's beneficence, within an artery of the Great Goddess.

Quite intoxicated, I linger until the shadow of the bridge stretches its long finger across me and reluctantly ease myself out of the water. The air has cooled slightly, but for just a moment, dripping and quite unveiled, I stand on the bank and stretch my arms out to the sky, full of vitality and saturated with sheer joy. The pleasures of solitude are unparalleled.

The moor remains deserted; I am soon dried by the late sun and, now decently dressed, make a slow and tranquil journey home. An owl calls from the woods..'toowit' - there is a pause and then from a distant tree I hear 'twoo'. A male has called for a mate and she has responded. Ain't love grand!

....

In the mellow evening light the barley field opposite sways rhythmically, revealing golden tints and dense ripe grain. Rustling in the breeze it tempts me with its whispering and I stroll across the lane, climbing the bank for a closer inspection. The long ears are silky to touch and I absentmindedly fondle them with my fingers, knowing that in a day or two this field will be reduced to stubble. The wind picks up and blows in my face and I am inspired to take a last look at the fullness of summer from the slight hill at the top of the field. Slowly, savouring every last moment, I climb the incline, brushing the barley ears with my hands, feeling the stalks sway and caress my bare legs. The fragrance of the barley, the deep heat of the earth and the temperamental looking sky all combine to weave a spell of summer, to encapsulate that throbbing pulse of fecundity that now bursts through into every kernel and seed lying within the body of the Mother. On the crest of the hill I stand and sway in the gathering breeze, stretching out my arms in wild abandon at the glorious ripeness of the surrounding fields. Peace and Plenty................. This is what mankind yearns for in his heart and this year it has been achieved once more. We have indeed been blessed and the Goddess lies in full glory at our feet. A deep peace creeps over me and I turn for home, down the hill to my cottage, lying snugly in the valley. The season of Lughnasadh has passed for another year. Our thanks to the Goddess for Her bounty, our thanks for fruit and seed, sunshine and moonshine, beauty and wonder.

....

Horses stand like a Turner painting dappled with early Autumn sunshine idly flicking flies with their tails. Swallows and house martins begin to gather in the late afternoon, dotting the telephone wires like crochets. A deep mellow warmth lies everywhere, the result of months of sunshine. Yellow ragwort stands proudly alone in the last remnants of the meadow, eaten down to a bowling green finish. Willowherb and Loosestrife wave purple along the river bank, thistledown floats gently on the breeze. Already they are ploughing and in the distance the first tractor of the season breasts the hill. Dusty roads, dusty trees. The Goddess sighs in repletion 'I can do no more.'

The first rosehips shine scarlet on the briars. I pick several handfuls and take them home. When they are strung they make a delightful adornment for the mantel-beam. On my return journey I hear music coming from a farmyard, high up on a nearby hill. It is the headquarters of a fairly large apple growing concern which I know well - they are clearly having a party. Voices call across the air, shouts of laughter, there is a distinct aura of merriment. Musing on the occasion and thinking what a beautiful evening they have chosen for the event, I meander down the road listening to the background sounds of a band playing somewhere in amongst the trees no doubt.

Two days later I bump into Sukie, the Managing Director, and mention the party. 'What party?' she says. I am stupefied. I clearly heard all the music and the laughter, surely I can recognise a social gathering when I hear it? She gazes at me, waiting for an explanation but I turn away; I realize what has happened and could not possibly explain. In her abrupt fashion Sukie dismisses me, no doubt bracketing me with all the other eccentric and none-too-bright yokels she has to deal with. I ponder on my hallucinatory experience - what had I heard? where had it come from? There had clearly been a time-slip and I had heard something of the past or future.

Later I mention it to a neighbour. 'Oh' she says 'they often had parties up there in her mother's time, when her father was alive. Big gatherings, in the yard.'

....

There is a new moon in Pisces and the sun, now moved into Virgo, was eclipsed last night. Consequently the weather has changed sharply and we have blustery winds, cool temperatures and rain showers; the aromatic smell of woodsmoke fills the evening air. I go out to investigate a snuffling and scuffling in the garden and encounter a large male hedgehog purposefully making his way into the shed. There I keep a hay-filled box for the cat to sleep in, should she prefer to spend her nights al fresco, and it is to this cosy bunk that he is heading. It is clearly time for hibernation and my shed is the chosen venue for this year. I hesitate to intervene but with thoughts of Jester snuggling down happily, only to find herself pierced with hedgehog quills, I feel it necessary to take action and go to inspect further. Already the hedgehog has buried himself so successfully that he is not visible above the hay but I nevertheless pull out the box and gently evict him. This produces much drama - he is not accustomed to being thwarted, and with a great deal of huffing and snorting determinedly runs back into the shed and buries himself deeply into the box. Faced with such overwhelming instincts I submit and firmly close the door. Jester will have to make alternative arrangements this year, this hedgehog needs his sleep more than her.

....

Now the first mists of the season roll across the meadow at sunrise. Shot through with unearthly tints of dawn which highlight the swirling clouds within clouds, I lean across the garden gate and search for Faerie shapes or enchanted beings. With both lunar and solar shifts all will be in a state of flux in the underworld as they prepare for the start of the last of the Great Tides of the year. It is during these transitional periods that a glimpse of Faerie is possible......alas I am disappointed - perhaps at the autumn equinox I will have more success. As I turn to go a mangy looking dog fox lopes across the meadow and disappears.

....

The end of the month brings a long overdue visit from a friend. We are both students of the occult and spend the evening poring over our respective Tarot packs; I ask Jennie to lay out a spread for me. Nothing too grisly is revealed and I am relieved at this, my own meditations on the cards have proved to be somewhat inconclusive. Then she says: 'There is a problem with your diet, something disagrees with you and should be adjusted.' I ponder on this after she has left; my diet is wholesome and I am still fairly lean and mean for my age.

After several days I realize that this is the nudge I need to turn vegetarian. For a long time I have considered taking the step but, being something of a carnivore, have put it off. Now, however, I feel I must take the plunge and spend an evening listlessly turning the pages of a vegetarian cookbook. It all looks incredibly dreary but in between visions of luscious pork chops and beef gravy I too see animal carcasses hanging up in the back quarters of the butchers, spring lambs that live only six months, chickens crammed into cages, fighting for breath, on their way to be slaughtered. Not for me, not for a Faerie Witch who supports life and cherishes the animal kingdom, not for one who seeks to distance herself from barbarism.

Rather grimly I draw up a few menus and, firmly grasping the nettle, make a brief sortie to my neighbourhood shop to stock up on more suitable provisions. Then I settle the butcher's bill and confront the fishman with a regular weekly

100

order. A further benefit of living alone is that there is no one to complain about the food, if I want to live on nature's harvest then I can do so unmolested. I resolve to eat more apples and honey and perhaps dig a little vegetable patch next year.

The Pool

Do you remember long ago when we were still quite young?
Do you recall that summer heat and how the days seemed
  long?
We used to take the winding track that led to Peyton Hall
It followed close beside the stream and to the waterfall.

The stony path, the cattle grid, the gently chewing cows
Between the trees we found a pool 'neath overhanging boughs.
The sun was hot, the air was still, the water softly played.
The bustle of the village seemed very far away.

The water goddess sang her song, the insects danced in time
We gazed at our reflections, our thoughts were intertwined.
With one accord we shed our clothes and slipped into the mere
The ripples ran, we caught our breath, the pool was deep and
  clear.

Then it was that time stood still, we felt we'd come to rest
In nature's bed, with silken sheets our bodies were caressed.
A calm seductive silence embraced our weary minds
Adrift in that enchanted pool our cares were far behind.

Innocent and sanguine we faced the throbbing sun
Floating naked, limbs outstretched, the two of us as one.
And when the shadows lengthened and our watery bed grew
  cold
We'd seek the refuge of the bank and watch twilight unfold.
Reluctant to relinquish the freedom and the peace

We'd linger in the meadow 'till the moon rose in the east.
Then exhilarated, captivated, our hearts restored and whole
We'd take our bodies homeward, behind us lay our souls.

If every I am lonely, downtrodden or oppressed
I conjure up the memory of those days that seemed so blessed.
And if I ever wonder what lovers find to do
I remember summer meadows and the days I spent with you.

September

A warm breeze, dry ploughed fields, long shadows and trees that rustle to a different rhythm. The earth is warm but the air is cool. Hazelnuts are forming amongst the dry browning leaves, ivy is blooming and the elderberries are black and heavy, richly displayed on their red stalks. Thistledown everywhere, the world is looking seedy.

Starlings fall from the sky like cinders from a chimney pot, then re-assemble on the telegraph wires in long sombre lines. Hops strew the hedgerows, a startling lime green against a greying background.

Watercress is thick on the river, encroaching until the far bank is reached. Teasels stand tall and neat, utilitarian in their appearance. The swallows are still with us, congregating on the power lines, twittering with plans.

This evening I light the first fire of the season, more for cheerfulness than for warmth.

We now approach the Autumn Equinox, a significant time in the year when a fresh magical current sweeps in. This is neither a solar nor lunar festival but, as with the Vernal Equinox, a specific time of balance, a pivotal point in time - equal day and equal night. It seems appropriate to mark this with a small personal rite and I make plans to arrange this for the evening of 21st. September.

....

It is a warm, drowsy evening and I take my rowboat out onto the river. There won't be many more opportunities for this so I must make the most of it. The moor has a soft and dreamy air, seed heads and fading flowers thrusting their way up through the rough grass on the bank - the trees are looking dingy. I drift downstream with the tide making for the long stretch of water which runs between field and copse. Two mature swans and a handful of large grey tufted cygnets watch suspiciously from a distance. Slowly I turn the corner of the rhyne, dreamily viewing the now shadowy bank and the new crop of water plants already thrusting their way up towards the light. Straight ahead out of a misty grey-blue sky rises the most enormous full moon I have ever seen. I gaze in wonder at this luminescent orb, so transparent, so silvery and ethereal; it occurs to me that I am witnessing a rare phenomena - is anyone else out there viewing it with the same incredulity? I stand in the boat and see it visibly clear the horizon, pale cream and fragile, then I raise my arms in appreciation, stunned with the beauty of this sight. 'O Great Goddess, we are truly blessed.' Tears prick my eyes and I slip out of time for a while marvelling at this glorious full moon, aimlessly flowing with the current like the Lady of Shalott.

Whilst landing the boat I spy a large, fresh puffball and carry it home in triumph. When sliced and fried with egg and chips it makes an appetising supper.

....

We are blessed with fine weather, this day, this equinoctial point, and I feel that an outdoor venue would be in order. My garden is quite secluded and I have long ago learnt to perform rites without attracting attention. It is glorious out under the stars and I spend a happy time arranging an altar; my young apple tree is to be the focal point, its' fruit of course being sacred to the Goddess and its' tender boughs providing some shelter. Balance is such a rare and necessary commodity these days that a plea for its return is to be the main purpose of my rite.

Bearing this in mind I dress the altar with a set of scales using two identical candles and including the two halves of an apple, cut across to reveal the star-shaped core so like the pentagram. The altar cloth is shaded into light and dark, chalice and dish are placed at opposite ends - all is symmetry and harmony.

I bathe and change into my robe, brush my hair free and compose myself with a brief meditation. Then, carrying a single candle, I slip outside and begin by casting the circle and establishing the quarters.

This is a highly concentrated and moving ceremony, I believe passionately in the balancing of opposing forces - the male and female, the dark and the light. It is through the restoration of this balance that the world and its' inhabitants will find concord and the necessary basis for future progress. The yin yang sign is symbolic of this and I use this emblem as a focal point when I invoke the God and Goddess - improvising, speaking slowly and with great sincerity.

106

When I feel that the circle is suitably protected I use the scales as a centrepiece, placing weights one at a time on the tray as I make my plea for greater balance on all levels of consciousness. When it reaches equipoise I make a personal request in the same vein.

I pause for a long, long, time, contemplating the scales before me, re-assessing the needs of humankind, very much aware of a pervading sense of peace. There is no awesome moment, no sudden flash of insight, I am simply conscious of being an integral part of a smoothly rounded circle, complete and unified. The moment lasts, I feel myself blending with an indefinable essence and for a brief moment my soul touches infinity.

It is over - I am back in reality, winding up the rite and bidding farewell to the Guardians. Quite at peace and convinced that my appeal has at least been heard, I send out absent healing to the multitude of tortured souls who are unable to heal themselves. May they find just a glimpse of tranquillity, something to hold onto, a lifeline of hope.

The night has turned cold and I am glad to get back indoors to rest in front of the fire, quite drained but spiritually cleansed. That night I sleep deeply and dreamlessly, floating somewhere between here and eternity.

....

A glorious morning with the moon directly overhead at 7:30 a.m. sharply outlined in her last quarter. The sun makes long shadows on the meadow and illuminates the tips of trees, already autumn singed. In the distance stand rows of closely packed hay-rolls, piled one on another, ready to be taken into storage for winter fodder. Swallows still skim the surface of the field looking for insects and late cow parsley gives a lacy surface to the grass. Each day brings change and, with it the poignancy of loss, another flower has faded, another signal of impending autumn becomes apparent.

....

There is thick, low lying mist in the early mornings now. Bushes and shrubs are strewn with cobwebs and everywhere is an atmosphere of change, a shifting of the tides as summer mellows out and winter stands briskly on the threshold. Whilst walking down the lane this evening the first leaves chased me, rustling and whirling behind my feet. Thousands of starlings line the telegraph wires and clouds more fly past overhead, wave after wave of them heading north, perhaps to join some greater flock. The walnut tree is shedding its' fruit and I gather a large bagfull to take inside and use over the forthcoming winter. My neighbour is poking a bonfire, no doubt the first of many; of all symbols this is surely the most significant of the changing season, the single plume of smoke, the aromatic mixture of dry grasses and leaves and the contemplative expression of the stoker. He regards my walnuts and I in turn regard his bonfire - we are both involved in rites of passage, no words are necessary.

....

All the ploughing is done, the fields like neat corduroy patches, uniform in colour. The hedgerows are thick with blackberries and morning glory flowers which look a little like debutantes who have stayed too late at the ball. The willows, the first to burst into leaf, are now variegated in colour, the hazel is dying a sad death, everywhere else is a dull mid-green. The weather is mild, breathtaking views in the sunshine but gloomy and chill in the shadows. Hips and haws brighten the scene, squirrels abound, leaping from the topmost branches. On the river, the remains of meadowsweet and forget me not flourish but the water is stagnant. It is a calm evening with a soft blue-grey sky overhead. The umbelliferous is now only dry brown stalks and seed heads but the rushes have retained their summer green. In the distance I watch a group of ten or more swans as they cluster together, beadily watching me row downstream in the boat. On the way home I collect some peat blocks for my fuel store, the nights are rapidly drawing in and once more I can spend time star-gazing after supper.

....

Still, I am sleeping well, now that the weather is cooler. I have not dreamed of anything profound for some time and no longer ponder on my nights' activities upon waking. Tonight, however, I am in an entirely new place, a clear, real, scenario and in a restaurant with an attractive blonde businessman who has a professional proposition to make. Somewhat flattered, I enjoy the main course and then, watching his face, like lightning, I 'see' the man behind the urbane mask. He is a procurer - not only am I intended for 'dessert' but I am destined for his shady little enterprise which involves a form of high class prostitution.

Appalled, I make an excuse to visit the ladies' loo and, once out in the empty foyer, head for the revolving doors which lead out onto the street. Alas, they are guarded by a nasty-looking henchman who looks at me knowingly - they had anticipated this. He stands menacingly in front of the doors watching me intently. Frantically I look for the stairs and see his counterpart guarding them also - there is no escape! Stunned into immobility I send up a passionate prayer for help and then.................and then........... I feel my own vibratory rate rise to an unprecedentedly high level and head blindly for the revolving doors. Simultaneously the two guards must have had theirs lowered for they move into slow motion and make clumsy, unhurried motions towards me, trying to bar the way. They appear drugged and disorientated. The doors too react in double-quick time and I am out and racing up the dark street at breakneck speed, my feet scarcely touching the pavement, able to run forever if need be.

I awake, my heart pounding. I am free, I have escaped, but the rhythm still runs through my veins and I sit up in bed contemplating the darkness of the small hours. This is no nightmare, this was real, I was in an astral realm quite close to the earth. A warning? A premonition? I lie there until dawn refusing to submit to panic but very, very wary.

For days I am haunted by this businessman - so clean-cut and professional, so well spoken and gentlemanly - a man one would be pleased to socialise with. I scrutinise all similar men who cross my path and cannot restrain my thumping heart when I encounter anyone who vaguely fits the description. Then I recall my prayers, my salvation from this near escape, and feel more secure. Within a week I have dismissed it from my mind; but on drifting off to sleep some time later I recall it vividly for some reason - there is to be a sequel. Sure enough, that night I enter the same realm, again quite real, but this time I am an invisible witness.

My businessman is having a massage in his bedroom, attended by a masseur and watched over by a Negro maid. All is luxury and opulence, there is no shortage of money as one would expect from a man of this background. Sitting on the floor, taunting him with threats of retribution if he should touch her, is a slim attractive coloured girl. Clearly she is here against her will and is intended for his use. Naively she pours scorn on his plans, sneering at his ignorance of the law, jibing him for his ignorance, singing a jaunty song to indicate her unconcern. I am shocked at her audacity and try to 'warn' her but of course it is in vain, I am unseen. She has failed to see that this is a man of power, a man of action with a lifetime of ruthlessness behind him. He says nothing, submitting to his masseur's experienced touch and she foolishly continues; the maid watches knowingly and I watch helplessly. Finally the massage is over and the blond businessman rises from the table, he walks across to the girl and with one swift movement propels her into the bedroom. A glass wall divides it from those of us remaining and we view a billowing four poster bed. Still taunting, she is roughly thrown onto the bed and we watch as she is systematically beaten, thrown across the bed, punched and pummelled until she is quite silent and probably dead. Tears fill my eyes - I knew he would do this - the other witnesses do not stir and I abruptly awake.

This is awful, why am I being 'shown' this? I am badly shaken, not only by the 'dream' but by the fact that I knew I was going to encounter him again. I search my memory but this man is a stranger to me here on the earth and I do not move in the circles where I might come across him. There is no more sleep that night and for days I am consumed by this horrifying vision, expecting to read of some racketeer being arrested for murder or a plea for a missing person. Those who are envious of psychic skills must surely be unaware of just how shocking they can sometimes prove to be.

The days pass and I settle down once more, pushing it all to the back of my mind - I do not 'see' him again and I turn my attention to the world around me.

After Dark

Once more the sun sinks slowly in the west
And birds enfold their young with feathered breast.
Probing shadows startle cottage doors
And weary men seek rest from daily chores.

The sudden dropping darkness of the night
Conceals a hooting owl on hunting flight.
A rising moon displays her glittering arc
Poised to guide those wanderers in the dark.

An evening mist rolls over field and lake
Muffling all that lies within its wake.
Softly breathing ageless lullabies
Until the earth submits with sleepy sighs.

Then a moment's pause, a silent breath
The shifting scene shows life beyond the death.
Twilight shapes emerge from near and far
And whispering comrades dance beneath the stars.

Faerie rules this secret dusky place
No mortal man can summon Nature's grace.
Only those who speak with earth and skies
Can find their way to where the Goddess lies.

And yet the call can oft-times penetrate
The gulf between the fey and human state
A chord is struck and Man may lift his head
Sensing ancient memories long since dead.

Though hill and wood may tempt his inner soul
Nocturnal stirrings rise and take control.
A cosy fireside holds him sure and fast
Subdues desire for nightly splendours past.

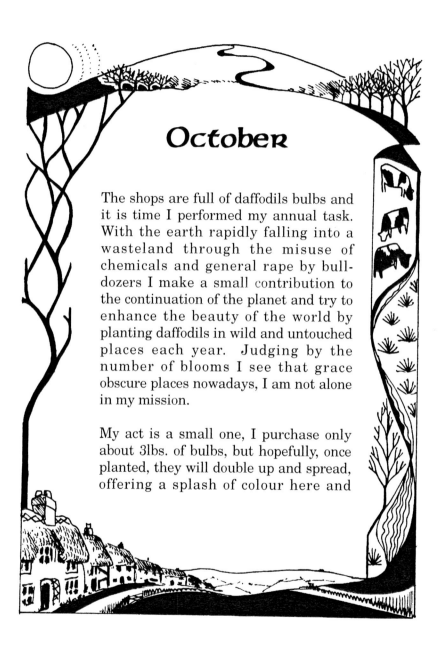

October

The shops are full of daffodils bulbs and it is time I performed my annual task. With the earth rapidly falling into a wasteland through the misuse of chemicals and general rape by bulldozers I make a small contribution to the continuation of the planet and try to enhance the beauty of the world by planting daffodils in wild and untouched places each year. Judging by the number of blooms I see that grace obscure places nowadays, I am not alone in my mission.

My act is a small one, I purchase only about 3lbs. of bulbs, but hopefully, once planted, they will double up and spread, offering a splash of colour here and

there, ushering in the Spring on windy March days. In the past I have often misplaced them, unwittingly planted beside tracks used by heavy vehicles which have squashed them to oblivion or under hedgerows where they have been nibbled by grazing sheep before they reach maturity. Now I take a little more care and choose my site well in advance after a preliminary survey.

This year I decide on a nature reserve to ensure the necessary protection for my plantings and on this cold, grey day, with rain in the wind I trudge along the riverside tow path, trowel in hand. The job itself gives no pleasure but here is a peat moor and the rich, friable, soil moves easily under my trowel. In no time I have planted the bulbs and firmed them down with a heavy tread. Two elderly ladies taking a brisk constitutional look at me quizzically but are too polite to enquire what I am doing. I don't spare a thought for the Ranger, he is nowhere to be seen and if he doesn't appreciate my daffodils in the Spring then he is no countryman. Satisfied with my deed I trudge back to the car, the trowel concealed under my coat.

....

Autumn dampness has settled in now and overcast skies and rain showers ensure that nowhere is really dry. The days are warm however and the trees still hold their leaves, green but faded. Blackberries glisten in the hedgerows and brambles as thick as my wrist choke and strangle. On a meandering journey through country lanes I pick pounds of rosehips in order to make wine and am delighted to still find great wreaths of hops cascading across the hedgerows which I gladly harvest and take home to decorate my beams and mantel. The swallows have gone - flown away one day when no one was looking. Virginia Creeper has turned red and glows from walls and trellises everywhere, more vivid than any summer climbing plant.

....

As we approach the feast of All Hallows I am given to periods of reflection on the magical year that is passing. We have seen the Goddess arise at Imbolc, flower at Beltaine and fruit at Lughnasadh. As her priestess and sworn witch I have followed Her progress with body and soul, linking with Her on seen and unseen levels, glorying in Her abundance and solemnly mourning Her demise. The God, now the Holly King, is making His presence felt and, as we say both farewell and welcome, I am anxious to make their acquaintance at this moment when the gates of the arcane world briefly swing open onto the mundane world. Consequently I have planned a small rite dedicated to Faerie, to the Lord and Lady of Life.

In my present frame of mind which is abstracted and creative, I do not find it difficult to write an appropriate ritual to be performed by seven people. In fact I have a feeling of compulsion and am aware of a nudging insistence - perhaps an otherworldly prod to make a magical contact through sacred drama. An idea develops based on an encounter with the Faerie King and Faerie Queen by 'material man' - the folk hero of our age -the ambitious businessman who gains great material wealth but loses his soul in the process. The setting is, of course, the greenwood and the labyrinthine trail that leads to the sacred centre where we face our real self, our alter ego - in this case the abandoned soul.

For several evenings I scribble away in front of the fire, ideas presenting themselves with great clarity, words flowing in a tumbling stream. When the script is complete I cast around for suitable participants and start the dreary round of telephoning friends. Six experienced ritualists are hard to find and the prospect of performing in a sacred drama brings out the primadonna in even the most dedicated magicians. I refuse to plead with any of them and trust in the Lord and Lady to prompt the right people into accepting. Eventually I

116

have a somewhat motley crew who
have agreed to support my
endeavours and we agree a date;
the venue is my home, small but
adequate. I scour the second hand
shops for a gown to use as a robe and am
suitably rewarded. Washed, ironed and
embellished, this pale green caftan will do very
well and my garland of honesty pods should
complete the outfit.

....

Now a beautiful warm day, calm on the river, and I spend an
hour rowing in peaceful contemplation of the changing scene;
then I land the boat and wrap it up for the winter - always a
poignant moment. Back home with armfuls of peat I stoke up
the woodburner, it will stay in now until late Spring and be a
focal point for my meditations and seer-ship. There is
something very significant and a little challenging about this
period in time; the Pleiades are visible on the eastern horizon
and we are now truly under the domain of the God, the
somewhat harsh masculine rule - death rather than life, cold
rather than warmth, gloom rather than colour.

....

A pall of mist lies across the meadow this morning, hinting at
Faerie enchantments and unseen beings. Otherwise it is
clear and bright with a light frost which has enhanced the
autumn colours of the remaining leaves - willows and poplars
have been stripped. It is too damp to meditate in the woods
but I nevertheless go for a ramble and find several stinkcaps
and other fungi thrusting their way through the leaf mold.
Back home I harvest quantities of dried honesty pods,
scattering the seed for another year. When I have constructed
a large display I find I have enough left over for a garland

and, with silver spray paint and ribbon manage a very delicate arrangement which will make a suitable head-dress.

....

Tonight is Hallowe'en and we gather for our Faerie Rite. Since the initial plans were made my dream life has been surprisingly fertile once more and my waking hours have been tinged with a somewhat otherworldly vagueness. Although the groundwork was completed some time ago I have been pre-occupied with Faerie during the intervening period; this has been more than mere anticipation - enchanted or enraptured perhaps. My colleagues are considerably less enthusiastic than I and there is a regrettable sense of grudging duty present when we assemble. Nevertheless everyone is suitably robed and petty rivalries are quelled as we congregate in the hallway before entering the living room which is to be our 'temple' or woodland glade for the evening.

We stand in sober silence for a few minutes, an air of expectancy replacing the somewhat negative undercurrents which previously dominated the atmosphere. My brow chakra is well open and I feel myself somewhat isolated from the rather prosaic thoughts emanating from the others. An opportunity to approach the Gods in a sacred manner such as this fills me with rapture, no matter what the circumstances - I feel myself beginning to drift. This is the first event I have arranged single-handedly and I truly hope that they will lend an ear to our humble offering and perhaps honour us with their presence.

Silence... total concentration, a withdrawing to that holy place within, and then slowly we start to process into the living room, walking sedately in accordance with the background music, candles in our hands illuminating the darkness, circling, circling until a 'faerie ring' has been described and we find ourselves in our pre-determined places.

There is a further pause for meditation and I sense an increasing commitment from the group as a whole, the circle has united us, the flickering candles focus our attention and, as a result, we relax and submit to whatever higher powers care to join us. At the appropriate moment I invoke the Faerie Queen and immediately afterwards Colin invokes the Faerie King. We pause in silence once more, allowing the words to take effect, and then begin the drama itself, scripts rustling as we search for our lines.

As ritual dramas go our's progresses fairly smoothly, the sobriety of the occasion bringing out the best in almost everyone. Under normal circumstances I would have been offended by the somewhat cynical and casual attitude of two male participants but I tell myself that it is simply masking their childish insecurities and refuse to be undermined. Consequently my initial budding rapture develops as I concentrate more fully on the words and movement, lights and music. I move into a trance-like state and as Colin and I circle with communion find myself exalted and quite uncaring of anything other than the passing moment.

Finally Colin and I meet at the central altar and offer communion to each other. I am trembling with the beginnings of ecstasy, an all too familiar passion, and Colin, inexperienced in these matters, mutters a word of rebuke. Suddenly, like a descending cloud I feel enclosed in an unfamiliar force field. There is a gasp from the onlookers and I submit to an invisible power that lifts my soul, cradles me in unseen arms and holds me in a state of spiritual suspension. Colin looks on in astonishment, wordlessly swallowing his criticism. My mind continues to float upwards until I feel almost weightless, the external world becomes distant and I am swimming in a fathomless sea of the soul. My colleagues appear dense and remote, their movements and whispers are meaningless; within this ethereal cloud all is stillness and refined essence, I am cocooned within a Faerie fascination.

In spite of this I find that I am able to function on the material plane and we, somewhat haltingly, conclude the rite; still the spell holds and we are one and all subdued and overwhelmed. Back in the hallway there is a revival of energy and much cheerful chatter ensues. I escape to the kitchen, still floating, still very much in two worlds, operating mechanically on the temporal plane but inwardly treading paths of enchantment, amazed, ecstatic and quite above it all. What is happening? Who is with me?

There is no doubt that our ritual has been successful and the Lord and Lady have given their unreserved blessing. As we gather round for a celebratory meal I am struck by everyone's tight grip on reality, an intense desire to remain earthbound through purposeful socialising, perhaps a denial of the power we have invoked. Real magic has been made this day - the doors between he worlds have swung open to reveal a glimpse of a higher reality and one of our number has been visibly sanctified. Yet, in spite of this, in spite of our joint success, our lifting of the veil, our momentary transcendence, I see only priests and priestesses wolfing down food and brightly chattering of everyday affairs. Where is their sense of wonder, their mystical awe?

I drift into the garden, still spellbound. Starlight gleams through the darkness and a glowing Hunter's moon bathes the land in glittering splendour. I offer my sincere thanks to the Lord and Lady of Life, the Faerie King and Queen, knowing that my gratitude can never be fully expressed. Still suspended in a timeless web of Faerie, the mundane world a faded backdrop, I am filled with a naked longing for a permanent place here, away from the gross materialism which is my daily lot. This, of course, will not be granted to me for many years to come and it is with a sense of sadness that I return indoors to my gossiping guests.

A plate of food has been left for me - food left out for the Faeries? Reluctantly I nibble at a sandwich and feel my spirit slowly returning to my body. Within a few minutes I am well and truly anchored, all contact broken, the world back in focus. There is nothing to do but utter a deep, deep sigh of regret.

In the deepest depths of my soul I knew that They would be at the rite - the rite that 'WE wrote' whispers a voice in my mind - I always knew.

Brick Kiln Hill

When the moon is full and glowing in the sky
When everyone's in bed 'cept you and I
We'll don our coats and lift the latch
Creep past dwellings warm with thatch
And climb up Brick Kiln Hill

When the Autumn mists lie cold above the ground
When dropping leaves remain the only sound
We'll leave our fireside - slip away
With muffled tread we'll forge our way
And climb up Brick Kiln Hill

We'll take the roadway, silent and benign
No traffic now, the world is yours and mine
Our lunar beacon gently guides us
Rustling hedgerows lie beside us
And climb up Brick Kiln Hill.

We'll leave behind the sleepy hamlet
The huddled houses snug and lamplit
Before us lies the road a-winding
Sharply shadowed, grey, spellbinding
The climb up Brick Kiln Hill.

Now all we hear are softly breathing cows
The night is still, afar a shrieking owl.
Trees stand sentry, guard us, greet us
Closer now the summit meets us
The top of Brick Kiln Hill.

Now at last we've reached our journey's end.
Stars above, behind the road descends.
Meadows, brooks and woods below
Bathed in silvery shadows glow
The top of Brick Kiln Hill.

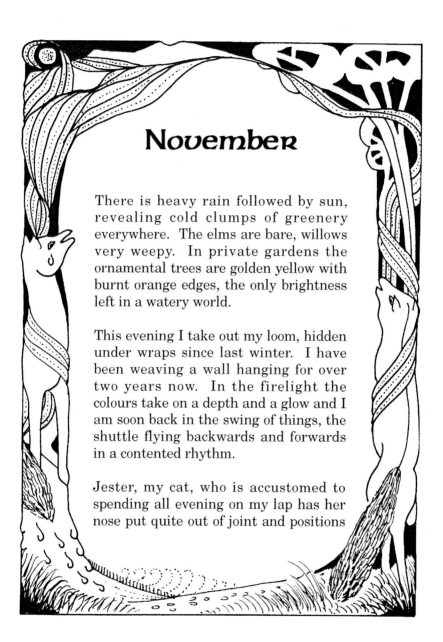

November

There is heavy rain followed by sun, revealing cold clumps of greenery everywhere. The elms are bare, willows very weepy. In private gardens the ornamental trees are golden yellow with burnt orange edges, the only brightness left in a watery world.

This evening I take out my loom, hidden under wraps since last winter. I have been weaving a wall hanging for over two years now. In the firelight the colours take on a depth and a glow and I am soon back in the swing of things, the shuttle flying backwards and forwards in a contented rhythm.

Jester, my cat, who is accustomed to spending all evening on my lap has her nose put quite out of joint and positions

herself as close to the loom as possible, showing her disapproval with slowly waving tail and an air of condemnation.

....

We have had a wild, wild night. Drenching rain has brought flooding, a lazy moon cradled in clouds graces the sky, the fields glow silvery in the moonlight; rivers have burst their banks and everywhere we wade through standing water. Autumn hedgecutting has begun.

....

I am settling in to the long dark evenings, either gazing mindlessly into the firelight or weaving at my loom. Tonight I find Jester sitting in the dead centre of my unwoven tapestry, registering quite clearly just what she thinks of my inattention to her. I am annoyed at her presumption and heave her off unceremoniously, whereupon she retires to the kitchen to sulk and I am able to weave in peace - she is a spoilt girl but it's too late to change things now. I hear the catflap bang loudly, she has slapped out in disgust. Before bedtime I uncork a bottle of last year's dandelion wine and taste the contents. As usual I have made it too sweet but it is still fairly palatable and I can look forward to a nightcap each evening now until the Spring.

....

Today I attend a gathering of like-minded souls in a nearby town for a rite. We are a Mystery School, scattered throughout the country and therefore only able to meet occasionally. Our backgrounds are all pagan but diverse in their nature, drawing from the ancient worlds of Greece, Crete, Ireland and of course Egypt on which we chiefly focus. Today, however, we are performing a ritual, or really a mass based on the

Greek Orthodox creed and the tone is Byzantine. Accordingly, we arrive ready to adorn ourselves in that period; the robes are impressively elaborate and the venue, a pavilion, gives us the privacy we need within an attractive setting.

After a long absence we greet each other warmly and there is much catching up on news and gossip. We are being given stage directions and a brief introductory talk by our High Priestess and then we move into position to begin the rite. It has been written by one of our members and is extremely moving in its rhythm and resonance. I am carried along by the beauty of the words and the cadence of the responses, priest, priestess and congregation harmoniously weaving a sacramental web. We are offered communion and shortly afterwards I look up to the far end of the room sliding effort-lessly into right brain mode. Transfixed I gaze dumbly upward and there, hovering over the altar is the winged Isis, vague, ephemeral but unmistakably She. I am overwhelmed with emotion, longing to exclaim and point but unable to and unwilling to break the spell with such mundane actions. Within moments the vision has faded and I finish the rite mechanically and breathlessly.

There is confusion and excitement afterwards but it is only the tension breaking, clearly no one else has seen our visitor. I beat a hasty retreat in order to mull over this phenomena, not a unique event by any means, but one which takes some digesting. Even now, as I write these words so many moons onward, the memory haunts me and my spirit surges in recollection.

....

Life settles back into routine and I take a Saturday job selling arts and crafts in a shop devoted to Wicca and the Goddess. The goods are tasteful and the customers varied; I meet many kindred spirits and a variety of artists, which inspires some interesting conversations. Soon I recognise the regulars and feel I am making friends. An attractive blond man comes in once or twice and shows an interest in a particularly expensive statue of Isis; he tells me that his maid broke an earlier one he purchased. We chat for a while - he is an educated man with some knowledge of the ancient world which somewhat contradicts his urbane and businesslike air. I am struck by his charm and good looks. Eventually he leaves without buying but returns two hours later, taking up the threads of our earlier conversation and deciding to buy the statue after all. As I wrap the item I am very much aware that he is leading up to an invitation, but he is diverted by the shop filling up with customers and our tête-a-tête is curtailed. Somehow he seems very familiar - perhaps he has been here before. Pondering, I take refuge in my innate reserve and finish the sale in a businesslike manner. Then he leaves and I turn my attention to the other customers.

Ten minutes later I slip out for some supplies, still musing on this attractive man who was so easy to talk to. As I cross the road I am suddenly thunderstruck, stopping in my tracks, causing a hold-up in the traffic. This is the man of my visions two or three months ago! This is the blond businessman who invited me out to dinner, who brutally beat up that poor girl, the superficially suave procurer with an ulterior motive, the man with the 'maid who broke my other statue'. Horns start honking as I stand rooted to the spot, my mouth hanging open, my eyes glazed. I cross the road and make for the market cross where I find a perch amidst the throng of Saturday afternoon shopper, my knees rapidly giving way. There I sit mutely staring into space, oblivious of the crowds, seeing only this man, and my earlier visions, very much aware of a near escape. Pictures race across the forefront of my mind, the taunting girl, the brutal beating, the two henchmen anticipating my escape from the restaurant. I am unaware of my surroundings, lost in the memory of my dreams, so real at the time and now horribly real once more.

There is no doubt that I was being warned with a vengeance, terribly warned. When I am at last able to collect my thoughts I feel quite resolute, this man no longer frightens me, nor does he attract me with his winning ways. Whatever his conscious persona his unconscious, shadow self has been revealed to me and I am unharmed. Now quite alert, I make my way back to the shop, aware that I had been quite prepared to succumb to his charms and respond to an invitation if it had been issued. Not now. Once more I thank those who are protecting me. Although freshly armoured and very much on guard I never see the blond businessman again.

A week later, I am nursing a damaged right hand, painfully bruised from a session in the garden. There is a knock at the door and I open it to reveal a tall, middle aged woman seeking directions. Apologising for my disability, I do my best to assist and to my astonishment she offers me healing. The pain is too great too refuse and she gently holds my injured hand between hers. Full of mutual gratitude we part company and an hour or so later I find that my hand is back to normal. Pondering on this angel of mercy, I remember where I have seen her before - she was the victim of an asthmatic attack at the Firewalk whom I had healed. All things come full circle - the Lords of Karma do indeed watch over us.

Night Fog

Night fog is made for barking dogs
To call from hill to glen
When silence hangs in tiny drops
And time has ceased for men.

Then through the gauzy curtain comes
A challenge and a dare
Returned by fellow watchdog from
Some distant farmyard lair.

The dog fox in the shrouded wood
His voice will also rise
Primeval are the forces
That stir these lonely cries.

Some long forgotten instinct seems
To gather in the pack
Recalling dark and dripping swamps
And savage forest tracks.

No more the hunt, no more the chase
The wild and hungry fights
Are now just foggy memories
Of ancient canine nights.

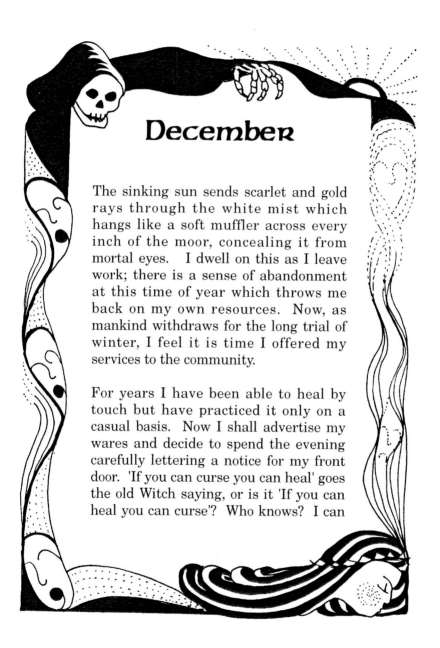

December

The sinking sun sends scarlet and gold rays through the white mist which hangs like a soft muffler across every inch of the moor, concealing it from mortal eyes. I dwell on this as I leave work; there is a sense of abandonment at this time of year which throws me back on my own resources. Now, as mankind withdraws for the long trial of winter, I feel it is time I offered my services to the community.

For years I have been able to heal by touch but have practiced it only on a casual basis. Now I shall advertise my wares and decide to spend the evening carefully lettering a notice for my front door. 'If you can curse you can heal' goes the old Witch saying, or is it 'If you can heal you can curse'? Who knows? I can think of several people I'd like to curse but shall refrain, the law of threefold return is a great deterrent, not to mention my future place in the Summerlands; I don't wish to affect my 'pension' because of a desire for sweet revenge. The sign looks well when put in place, however it is so remote here I wonder if I shall have any customers. No doubt the Gods will direct the appropriate patients to my door.

An Anglo Saxon Curse:

'May you be consumed as coal upon the hearth
May you shrink as dung upon a wall
And may you dry up as water in a pail
May you become as small as a linseed grain
And much smaller than the hip bone of an itch mite
And may you become so small that you become nothing.'

DELICIOUS!

Whilst signing cheques in the office today Ralph, our M.D. breaks his gold pen. He hurls it across the office in disgust and storms out looking for a fight with one of the factory hands. The spellworking has run its' course.

The full moon is beginning to wane and we have cold, clear, midnight blue skies; every chimney is sending out a plume of smoke and there is frost underfoot. All the trees are bare now. The cat has de-camped to the airing cupboard for the winter.

Whilst wandering aimlessly down the hallway I absent-mindedly catch sight of myself in the mirror. Who is this creature I so seldom survey? I move in more closely and observe a new, radiant being - the skin, once sallow and distinctly eggshell in texture, is now glowing with colour and shining with a satin finish. The hair gleams and I even spy a curl or two, peeping out of previously lank but now quite abundant tresses. Somewhat vainly I smile at my reflection and shake my hair about like a teenager; there is no doubt about it, I am looking extremely well and revitalized. Four months of vegetarianism has had an effect. I have taken Jennie's advice and purged myself of the toxins carried by a meat diet: the result is a vastly improved complexion and hair that belongs more to the maiden than the crone. Very pleased with this discovery I put all thoughts of bacon sandwiches behind me forever, there will be no more dead animals on my behalf. I just hope my insides are are squeaky clean as my outside.

....

It is the winter solstice, death and decay lie all around us in sombre silence. The sky is overcast, pale indigo with silver streaks at early twilight. Vegetation is unidentifiable, clumped and sodden, only the menacing nettles emerge from this desolation. After dark I venture out for a last look at this wintry world and discover a crystal clear, star studded sky - it is breathtaking in its beauty, a scene I never tire of. Directly overhead lie the Plieades, proclaiming midwinter by their position as they have done for thousands of years. In spite of turmoil and strife here on our little planet one feels that God is indeed in His heaven and the universal clock is unmoved by our human peccadilloes.

Back inside I light a large white candle and wreath it in holly and ivy. It will burn now each evening for a few hours during the dark days that we are passing through until the tides shift and the days start to extend. In this deep, chasmic gloom I do not feel celebratory but wish instead to keep a pinprick of light burning. In the candlelight I hold my hand over my heart and repeat the old Irish evening prayer.

'May the light of lights come
To my dark heart from thy place.
May the spirit's wisdom come
To my heart's tablet from Dana.

Deep peace of the running wave to me
Deep peace of the silent stars
Deep peace of the flowing air to me
Deep peace of the quiet earth.
May peace, may peace, may peace, fill my soul.
Let peace, let peace, let peace make me whole.'

This is my midwinter rite - soothing, quiet and underlined with hope. A light in the midst of darkness.

At Yule I burn a traditional log and toast the season with some home-made wine. Mistletoe, that old sacred herb, hangs in a ball from one of the beams. Out in the cold, frosty air I throw bread for the hungry birds and break the ice on the birdbath ready for drinking.

....

There is an exquisite sunrise this morning; long fingers of orange, red and pink light up the sky from horizon to horizon. Stratus clouds are flushed rapidly from smoky blue to a soft rose shade and the frost underfoot is illuminated and transformed into a sparkling crystalline carpet. A narrow waning Gemini moon slips out of sight in the west.

I sense a subtle shift from the inertia of midwinter - the tide is beginning to turn, and there is a glimmer of hope in the midst of this cold stagnation. Shivering with cold I stand at the garden gate and open up my senses to the Greater Whole - yes the pivotal point has been reached and breached, the God has started to lose his power, the Goddess will soon stir and resurrect herself. There is a faint whisper of promise. With this comforting thought in mind I reluctantly leave my vantage point and go back indoors. Another year lies ahead, another clean strip of parchment on which to inscribe and decorate a further chapter of our lives.

Death Throes

Faintly, faintly, sun glows in the skies
Slowly, slowly, struggling hard to rise
Avid death claws wildly at the earth
Suffocating whispers of rebirth

Sinking, sinking, crawling o'er the rim
Fading, fading, light and fire grow dim
Creeping torpor silently unfolds
Life withdraws and sleep restores her hold.

Crying, crying, bleakly pagans plea
Flowing, flowing, breath and blood ebb free
December tides strew embers in their wake
And winter winds complete the final break.

Draining, draining, souls release their grip
Mourning, mourning, skeletally stripped.
Man suspends his pulse whilst nature rests
The Goddess turns Her face, no more to bless.

FREE DETAILED CATALOGUE

Capall Bann is owned and run by people actively involved in many of the areas in which we publish. A detailed illustrated catalogue is available on request, SAE or International Postal Coupon appreciated. **Titles can be ordered direct from Capall Bann, post free in the UK** (cheque or PO with order) or from good bookshops and specialist outlets.

Do contact us for details on the latest releases at: **Capall Bann Publishing, Freshfields, Chieveley, Berks, RG20 8TF.** Titles include:

Angels and Goddesses - Celtic Christianity & Paganism, M. Howard
Arthur - The Legend Unveiled, C Johnson & E Lung
Auguries and Omens - The Magical Lore of Birds, Yvonne Aburrow
Asyniur - Womens Mysteries in the Northern Tradition, S McGrath
Beginnings - Geomancy, Builder's Rites & Electional Astrology in the
    European Tradition, Nigel Pennick
Between Earth and Sky, Julia Day
Caer Sidhe - Celtic Astrology and Astronomy, Michael Bayley
Call of the Horned Piper, Nigel Jackson
Cat's Company, Ann Walker
Celtic Faery Shamanism, Catrin James
Celtic Lore & Druidic Ritual, Rhiannon Ryall
Celtic Sacrifice - Pre Christian Ritual & Religion, Marion Pearce
Celtic Saints and the Glastonbury Zodiac, Mary Caine
Circle and the Square, Jack Gale
Compleat Vampyre - The Vampyre Shaman, Nigel Jackson
Creating Form From the Mist - The Wisdom of Women in Celtic Myth and
    Culture, Lynne Sinclair-Wood
Crystal Doorways, Simon & Sue Lilly
Crossing the Borderlines - Guising, Masking & Ritual Animal Disguise in the
    European Tradition, Nigel Pennick
Earth Dance - A Year of Pagan Rituals, Jan Brodie
Earth Harmony - Places of Power, Holiness & Healing, Nigel Pennick
Earth Magic, Margaret McArthur
Eildon Tree (The) Romany Language & Lore, Michael Hoadley
Enchanted Forest - The Magical Lore of Trees, Yvonne Aburrow
Eternal Priestess, Sage Weston
Eternally Yours Faithfully, Roy Radford & Evelyn Gregory
Everything You Always Wanted To Know About Your Body, But So Far
    Nobody's Been Able To Tell You, Chris Thomas & D Baker
Face of the Deep - Healing Body & Soul, Penny Allen

Fairies in the Irish Tradition, Molly Gowen
Familiars - Animal Powers of Britain, Anna Franklin
Forest Paths - Tree Divination, Brian Harrison, Ill. S. Rouse
Gardening For Wildlife Ron Wilson
Goddesses, Guardians & Groves, Jack Gale
Handbook For Pagan Healers, Liz Joan
Handbook of Fairies, Ronan Coghlan
Healing Book, The, Chris Thomas and Diane Baker
Healing Homes, Jennifer Dent
Healing Journeys, Paul Williamson
Healing Stones, Sue Philips
Herb Craft - Shamanic & Ritual Use of Herbs, Lavender & Franklin
In Search of Herne the Hunter, Eric Fitch
Inner Celtia, Alan Richardson & David Annwn
Inner Mysteries of the Goths, Nigel Pennick
Inner Space Workbook - Develop Thru Tarot, C Summers & J Vayne
Intuitive Journey, Ann Walker Isis - African Queen, Akkadia Ford
Journey Home, The, Chris Thomas
Kecks, Keddles & Kesh - Celtic Lang & The Cog Almanac, Bayley
Language of the Psycards, Berenice
Lid Off the Cauldron, Patricia Crowther
Light From the Shadows - Modern Traditional Witchcraft, Gwyn
Magic of Herbs - A Complete Home Herbal, Rhiannon Ryall
Magical Guardians - Exploring the Spirit and Nature of Trees, Philip Heselton
Magical History of the Horse, Janet Farrar & Virginia Russell
Magical Lore of Animals, Yvonne Aburrow
Magical Lore of Cats, Marion Davies
Magical Lore of Herbs, Marion Davies
Magick Without Peers, Ariadne Rainbird & David Rankine
Masks of Misrule - Horned God & His Cult in Europe, Nigel Jackson
Medium Rare - Reminiscences of a Clairvoyant, Muriel Renard
Mind Massage - 60 Creative Visualisations, Marlene Maundrill
Moon Mysteries, Jan Brodie
Mysteries of the Runes, Michael Howard
Mystic Life of Animals, Ann Walker
Pagan Feasts - Seasonal Food for the 8 Festivals, Franklin & Phillips
Patchwork of Magic - Living in a Pagan World, Julia Day
Pickingill Papers - The Origins of Gardnerian Wicca, Bill Liddell
Pillars of Tubal Cain, Nigel Jackson
Places of Pilgrimage and Healing, Adrian Cooper
Practical Divining, Richard Foord
Practical Meditation, Steve Hounsome
Psychic Self Defence - Real Solutions, Jan Brodie
Real Fairies, David Tame
Reality - How It Works & Why It Mostly Doesn't, Rik Dent
Romany Tapestry, Michael Houghton

Sacred Animals, Gordon MacLellan
Sacred Celtic Animals, Marion Davies, Ill. Simon Rouse
Sacred Dorset - On the Path of the Dragon, Peter Knight
Sacred Geometry, Nigel Pennick
Sacred Ring - Pagan Origins of British Folk Festivals, M. Howard
Season of Sorcery - On Becoming a Wisewoman, Poppy Palin
Seasonal Magic - Diary of a Village Witch, Paddy Slade
Secret Places of the Goddess, Philip Heselton
Secret Signs & Sigils, Nigel Pennick
Self Enlightenment, Mayan O'Brien
Spirits of the Air, Jaq D Hawkins
Spirits of the Earth, Jaq D Hawkins
Spirits of the Earth, Jaq D Hawkins
Stony Gaze, Investigating Celtic Heads John Billingsley
Stumbling Through the Undergrowth , Mark Kirwan-Heyhoe
Subterranean Kingdom, The, revised 2nd ed, Nigel Pennick
Symbols of Ancient Gods, Rhiannon Ryall
Talking to the Earth, Gordon MacLellan
Taming the Wolf - Full Moon Meditations, Steve Hounsome
Teachings of the Wisewomen, Rhiannon Ryall
The Other Kingdoms Speak, Helena Hawley
Tree: Essence of Healing, Simon & Sue Lilly
Tree: Essence, Spirit & Teacher, Simon & Sue Lilly
Torch and the Spear, Patrick Regan
Understanding Chaos Magic, Jaq D Hawkins
Warriors at the Edge of Time, Jan Fry
Water Witches, Tony Steele
Way of the Magus, Michael Howard
Weaving a Web of Magic, Rhiannon Ryall
West Country Wicca, Rhiannon Ryall
Wildwitch - The Craft of the Natural Psychic, Poppy Palin
Wildwood King , Philip Kane
Witches of Oz, Matthew & Julia Philips
Wondrous Land - The Faery Faith of Ireland by Dr Kay Mullin
Working With the Merlin, Geoff Hughes
Your Talking Pet, Ann Walker

FREE detailed catalogue and FREE 'Inspiration' magazine

Contact: Capall Bann Publishing, Freshfields, Chieveley, Berks, RG20 8TF